From Puzzles
to Portraits

THE JOHN W. HARRELSON LECTURES

THE JOHN W. HARRELSON LECTURES

*Through the generous bequest of the late
Chancellor J. W. Harrelson of North Carolina
State University at Raleigh, the Harrelson
Lectureship and Acquisitions were created
in 1961. Of the several objectives of this
fund, the Lectures have taken first priority
in the belief that the inspirational spark
generated by a distinguished scholar and
transmitted by personal contact with students,
faculty, and the general public adds significantly
to the intellectual growth of the community.
The present publication is a result of the
Harrelson Lectures for the 1968–69 academic year.*

From Puzzles
to Portraits

PROBLEMS OF A LITERARY BIOGRAPHER

by James L. Clifford

The University of North Carolina Press
Chapel Hill

Frontispiece drawing by Frank Holyfield

Preface ஜ At the start I should make clear what is intended in the present volume. Basically my approach is neither historical nor critical. I am a practicing biographer, and my concentration is wholly on the operative concerns of a writer who decides to re-create the career of another person. Admittedly, not many readers of this book will ever attempt such a project. But a discussion of what is involved should have some value for the everyday reader.

What exactly are the problems which face a literary biographer? In the first place there is the matter of finding all the relevant evidence. And once assembled, how does he use it? How does he combine the many pieces of his jigsaw puzzle into one finished portrait? What specifically are the choices he will have to make as to form and content? Are there any accepted rules which will tell him what to do? What kinds of pressures must he face? How many opinions of his own can he introduce into his work? How legitimate is it for him to psychoanalyze his subject? These matters, and many others, are discussed in the following pages. The emphasis is on working decisions and practical concerns, rather than theories or aesthetic values.

My excuse for being so detailed and technical in places is that until recently there has been very little genuine critical work on the art of biography. While the techniques of poetry, drama, or fiction have been widely discussed in hundreds of important books and articles, very little has been said about life-writing. One reason, perhaps, has been that until our day it has been undefined. Few have thought of it as a distinct literary genre. Most theorists have considered biography as a minor part of history, but not one which required much critical analysis. Everything was quite simple. The would-be biographer had merely to assemble what facts he could find, put them together end to end in chronological order, and that was that. What art might be involved was stylistic, the ability to tell the story smoothly and with grace. The biographer was merely a craftsman who served a useful purpose. But he should not, it was assumed, be considered more than that.

It is not my purpose here to trace the twentieth-century reaction to that traditional point of view—the insistence today on the "art" of biography—or the claims in some quarters that it should be thought of as a major literary genre. You will find these points argued cogently in the work of a number of our modern critics. I mention it only as a further justification of my basic approach. If life-writing can be considered as an art, then analysis of methods and techniques should be rewarding.

At the start, too, I must make a confession and an apology. Most of the first part is autobiographical—coming from my own experiences in writing three biographies—one of the friend and hostess of Samuel Johnson, Mrs. Thrale-Piozzi; another of his early life, *Young Sam Johnson*; and the last, not yet completed, which will describe Johnson's middle years. If such concentration on my own exploits and failures, on my decisions and compromises, seems blatantly egotistical, I cannot help it. These are what I know best. They could undoubtedly be duplicated from the records of any other practicing biographer, and I hope are truly representative. Should some readers wonder at the wealth of detail, especially for incidents occurring over thirty years ago, I may add that, while some come from vivid memories most of them are securely based on letters written at the time. I may, like Boswell, have occasionally expanded a short description into a dramatic scene, but I hope the account is no less authentic.

In the second part of the book I make no claim to having found solutions to the many trying problems—technical and ethical—which must be faced. I have no dependable methods of estimating the reliability of anecdotes, or of devising rules for their use. I have no basic ethical standards to suggest to the perplexed author, faced with powerful external pressures from the family and friends of his subject. But merely from a description of the many difficulties involved, and through an explanation of a few crucial cases, the reader should have a clearer notion of the complexity and subtlety of the whole process. What I hope will emerge is the delight and the anguish which inevitably come to every writer of biography.

Acknowledgments

Some portion of what follows was first given as the Harrelson Lectures at North Carolina State University at Raleigh in March, 1969. I am indebted to Professor Lodwick Hartley, whose idea it was in the first place, to Chancellor John Tyler Caldwell, Dr. Harry Kelly, Provost, and to Professor W. W. Kriegel and other members of the Harrelson Fund Committee. I wish to thank the following who at various times helped with valuable advice: Professor Richard D. Altick, Mr. John Carswell, Professor Leon Edel, Professor John A. Garraty, Professor Lodwick Hartley, Professor Edgar Johnson, Professor John H. Middendorf, Professor Maurice Quinlan, Mrs. Richard L. Hanson, and others mentioned in the text. Both for style and content my chief debt, as always, is to my wife, Virginia.

Contents

Part One
Finding the Evidence

I. "Outside" versus "Inside" Research

How does the biographer begin? Where does he find his material? Whom does he consult? While there are obviously no simple answers to such questions, one thing is certain. The work cannot all be done in the safe confines of a library.

I would be the last person to deprecate the reading of old books, or the importance of printed records. A biographer must start by absorbing all that has previously been written about his subject. He must consult the earlier studies and pore over old periodicals, as he gathers together all the known facts. He must use what manuscript material is available in rare book rooms of important libraries. He will have to spend long hours with musty volumes and work his way through piles of long-forgotten authorities. This is the popular conception of the biographical scholar. But there is another side to life-writing which I like to call "outside" research, as contrasted to "inside" work at a desk. This is the search for valuable new evidence not to be found in libraries. And the problems of this "outside" search are not so well known or so widely discussed. There are no authoritative handbooks that will provide all the answers for the beginning literary detective. Normally each worker is left to his own devices, or receives advice from more experienced practitioners.

What follows, then, is an informal account of some of my own adventures, which will show what fun the whole business can be. Most of them do not involve superior knowledge or wide acquaintance with special techniques; indeed most of my real successes, as you will see, have been solely the result of phenomenal luck. But even luck can sometimes be manipulated.

Before I begin my story, however, it may be worthwhile to make clear the vital importance of this "outside" research. Why, some readers may ask, spend so much time and energy hunting for more and more evidence about well-known people? For most modern subjects is there not sufficient printed evidence already available in our libraries? And in particular why spend years merely hunting for the originals of letters and documents already printed? To the first question I believe the answer is obvious. Everyone knows that the discovery of unknown and unpublished diaries and letters may throw new light on some perplexing interpretation. Though small in themselves, such discoveries may be of incalculable importance in a larger critical analysis. And there is no doubt that there is much more to be found.

The answer to the second question may not be so obvious. Why spend years searching for original manuscripts of material already in print? The reason may be categorically stated—many of the published versions are not dependable. At the risk of being immediately challenged, I would go so far as to insist that scarcely any volumes of letters or biographical material edited before the twentieth century can be implicitly trusted, either for accuracy of text or for completeness. After years of examining great numbers of older editions, I have yet to find any that I do not suspect of having been in some way tampered with. Of course, the degree of distortion varies enormously. In some nineteenth-century editions the offense may be venial, with only minor corrections of language and a few excisions, but the texts are not reproduced with the accuracy we demand today. For many editions the distortion is major. Only in our day do we begin to have complete editions, unexpurgated and unmanipulated, but the number is even now pitifully small. For the majority of subjects in the past we must still use authorities which we suspect. Until we can be sure that we are really getting accurate transcriptions of what the men and women of former centuries really thought and said, we cannot say that we know the past.

There are two sources for our mistrust of older editions: first, the original writers themselves; and second, the later editors. In the eighteenth century, for example, many literary figures rewrote their own letters with an eye to posterity, and the practice was more widespread than many realize. The name of Alexander Pope immediately springs to mind; yet Pope did only what scores of others were doing. Horace Walpole's long series of letters to Sir Horace Mann—what W. S. Lewis calls "the great Andean range of the Walpolian continent"—has been printed, even in the latest editions, not from the original letters (alas! probably destroyed), but from a transcript by Walpole, made with future readers in mind.[1] Many passages in the original letters may have been omitted, so that the version we have merely represents what the elder Walpole wished us to have, not what he actually wrote first. Lady Mary Wortley Montagu's fascinating letters from Turkey in their published form were not the ones originally sent back to England.[2] There are many other instances. Indeed, the more one works in the earlier periods, the more shocked he becomes at the amount of revising which went on.

Let me cite one other typical example—the letters of Anna Seward, the so-called "Swan of Lichfield." All through the nineteenth century and in the twentieth, one of the most quoted authorities about the Johnson group and the late Bluestockings has been the six-volume edition of her letters, which was published by Constable in 1811. Often reprinted have been some of her acid remarks about Dr. Johnson. Here, it has been suggested, is the unlovely side of the great Bear, seen through the eyes of an unsympathetic contemporary. But that edition of Miss Seward's correspondence, it is now clear, is not what Anna Seward wrote to her correspondents in the late eighteenth century. The printed text which has been the sole source of all succeeding editions of her correspondence represents a subsequent rewriting by Miss Seward herself, long after the letters had been sent. This is what happened. For twenty years at least she kept copies of her most important letters. Then as an old lady—impressed by what she considered her great importance as a literary figure—she decided to rewrite from these copies, for a published edition after her death. And Constable obligingly printed what she provided. Now fortunately some of her original letters have turned up, and in comparing the manuscripts with the printed text we unmask the culprit. Some startling changes are revealed. For example, most of the printed nasty remarks about Johnson do not appear in the originals written before 1791. But after reading Boswell's *Life of Johnson*, published that year, and feeling herself slighted in various ways, she decided to get her revenge by publishing revised versions of her earlier letters. By so doing she completely distorted the truth about what she had thought of Johnson while he was alive.[3]

The Johnsonian allusions are the only ones that I have personally checked, but if her other remarks were revised in a similar mood, we must be frankly skeptical when using any of her published letters. Even the dates, strangely enough, appear to have been tampered with, so that the correspondence cannot even be safely used for chronology.

Diaries also were often rewritten. We now know that Mme. D'Arblay as an old lady slashed up and revised portions of the famous diary she kept as Fanny Burney. Fortunately, it is usually called the D'Arblay diary, for it represents what the older woman wished to have preserved, not wholly what she had set down earlier. Yet it is the revised version which is always quoted, and almost never is there any reference to the fact that the evidence may be garbled. How badly needed is a new edition from the original manuscript![4]

Although later editors were not as active in rewriting manuscripts, they did what was just as bad; they selected, destroyed, bowdlerized, and eviscerated indiscriminately. In the eighteenth and nineteenth centuries editors thought nothing of cutting whole passages out of letters, leaving no marks whatsoever to indicate their omissions; of altering the dates; combining two or three notes from different years into a longer letter with a single date; and changing the wording to suit contemporary tastes.

When William Hayley printed some notes he had received from William Cowper, he was not averse to changing the actual content. In one letter of 4 June 1792, Cowper had referred to returning from a midday walk in June, puffing and blowing and steaming with perspiration. The whole description struck Hayley as being indecorous and so he invented a high wind, and altered the next passage to "Returned from my walk, blown to tatters—found two dear things in the study."[5]

Editors thought it their duty to search through long correspondences for anything that might inculcate morality and good manners, and to throw aside other letters which were filled with gossip or descriptions of everyday life. Thus the editor of the four-volume edition of the works of Mrs. Chapone (Hester Mulso) in 1807 admitted that he had been very selective,[6] and he chose certain epistles which presented Mrs. Chapone as a rather stuffy, moralizing sort of person. Unhappily she has come down to us in this guise. But where are the other letters, ignored by her first editor? What might they show us about the lady?

Typical of what an early nineteenth-century editor thought was his duty in preparing manuscripts for the press is the explanation given in the Preface to a four-volume edition of the letters of Elizabeth Carter and Catherine Talbot.[7] There the Rev. Montagu Pennington, Miss Carter's nephew, explains that throughout he has omitted most of the references to the health of Miss Carter, most of the anecdotes about the editor's own family, and all anecdotes about people still living. Moreover, he has always left out everything which he suspected Miss Carter herself would not have wished to see in print. Again he admits that he has joined many shorter notes together into one, for the ease of the reader. And throughout the edition there are no asterisks or other marks to indicate changes or omissions. Yet these volumes have ever since been used as a standard authority, and modern scholars calmly quote from them with no seeming awareness of their deficiencies. Someone must find the originals of these letters—another twentieth-century must!

These are a few random examples. If we want to know what actually occurred in former ages, we must never give up our healthy skepticism about every older published work. Too often modern biographers and critics have generalized from twisted facts. What I began by calling "outside research" becomes a serious demand for factual truth.

The search for authentic records will usually begin with attempts to track down remaining members of the subject's family. If this sounds simple, it is not always so, for gaining access to a son

or daughter, or granddaughter, or distant cousin, may prove difficult. Then there are business associates, or close personal friends,
with much to tell, or with forgotten papers stored away in an attic.
Persistence and hours of patient labor may be spent just in getting
in touch with them. There are no foolproof techniques or rules of
procedure for approaching the relatives of a famous man.[8] Inevitably one must work through hunches and sudden decisions. Looking
back, the researcher can often see how important chance has been
in his discoveries.

I could tell story after story of the role luck has played in a
biographer's career. Anna Kitchel of Vassar, for example, went to
England some years ago to search for material for a biography of
George Lewes, the husband of the novelist George Eliot. For most
of a year Miss Kitchel hunted and hunted, with no real success.
Near the end of her stay abroad she was one day riding on top of a
London bus, and complained bitterly to a friend of her failures. "I
would give anything," she is reputed to have said, "to find something really new about Lewes—just anything." A person sitting in
the seat just ahead turned around and said: "Would you like to see
his diaries?" Through this chance encounter on the bus Miss
Kitchel was able to meet Lewes's granddaughters and to consult
masses of his private papers.[9]

Another valuable chance meeting happened to Edgar Johnson,
when he was just beginning his biography of Sir Walter Scott. He
and his wife planned to go to Edinburgh to work in the National
Library of Scotland. It was just before Christmas, and the train,
The Royal Scot, was packed with vacationers. Their own compartment was filled with noisy young people, laughing and shout-
ing. At the first dinner call, most of them left for dinner, leaving
behind only the Johnsons and a lady more nearly their contemporary. She showed so openly her relief at their going—a relief
fully shared by the Johnsons—that a conversation ensued. What
was their astonishment when the lady turned out to be the half-
sister of the present members of the Scott family living at Abbotsford. She was on her way there to spend the holidays. They had a

pleasant talk, and later the Johnsons received an invitation to spend a weekend at Abbotsford. Thus they had a perfect introduction to the study of the Scott relics there. If the noisy holiday people had not left the compartment the Johnsons and the reticent lady in the corner would probably never have exchanged a word, and the opportunity might have been lost.

Almost any biographer could tell similar stories, some not so dramatic. In each instance, the fortunate result comes from mere chance and not careful planning. Leon Edel told me that just before World War II, when he was in Paris, he became friendly with a young French journalist, and dined with him fairly often. A pleasant relationship developed, having nothing to do with English literature. Later his friend suggested that he would like to have Edel meet his father, who had just retired and returned to Paris after having served as head of the French Institute in Florence. While Edel was lunching with the family, he chanced to look across the room to a shelf, with a row of books, and there spotted a copy of Henry James's *American Scene*—a bulky volume, with a red cover. "Oh," he blurted out in English (they had been speaking French). "I see you have James's *American Scene*." "Why, yes," his host replied. "It is a great book. James was a great writer." The conversation continued on James, and Edel finally remarked. "But you are talking as if you knew Henry James." His host replied, "I knew him for many years"; and then he told in detail about his first meeting with the novelist, and after lunch brought out a bundle of his letters. Edel had had no inkling whatsoever that the Mengin family had any connection with one of his major interests.

As one more example, in London in the autumn of 1951, when I was hard at work on my *Young Sam Johnson* I happened to meet a well-to-do business man named Francis Gaster, who had been a member of the London Johnson Society. As we chatted, he casually remarked that he had recently seen some original Johnson letters, but unhappily they were from his later years and thus of no use to me in my present project. He explained that he had gone out to Denham in Buckinghamshire to attend a village fete. In one room of the building where the celebration was being held there had been an exhibition of some local treasures. Although most of them scarcely interested him, he had been astonished to see pinned to the walls a few original letters of Dr. Johnson. As an admirer of the Doctor, he had recognized the signatures and been amused to find them exhibited in such a casual way. To be sure, he had only glanced at them and seen that they were dated in the 1780's. He knew no more than that. Whether they were well known or not, or whether they were in print, he had no idea. It was merely the startling fact of finding them pinned to a wall that had made a real impression.

It did certainly seem a bit odd, but then, anything can happen at a local fete. The more I thought about the matter the more curious I became. Even though these late letters were not related to my particular job of the moment, it would be useful to know the present ownership of all surviving correspondence. And who knew what else the owner might have? So I asked Mr. Gaster if he could find out more about the letters. A few weeks later he wrote that he had found out the name of the owner and suggested that we might drive out together to Gerrard's Cross the following Sunday. I at once accepted, and in the middle of November we had a pleasant drive out to call on a Major R. H. Way, of Badminton House, Marsham Way. We were graciously received and after the usual amenities our host spread out before us six short notes in the handwriting of Samuel Johnson. They were addressed to a Mrs. Way of Denham Place, an ancestress of the present owner.

I was frankly puzzled, for I did not remember any Mrs. Way as one of Johnson's friends, and the short letters rang no bell in my memory. Thus I had to confess that without checking in the library I could not tell whether these were known and printed or not. "Take them along, and check them," said our host. "But you don't know me," I stuttered, "how can you trust me with such valuable manuscripts?" "Oh, I'm sure that would be all right," he replied. Happily, Mr. Gaster, who had social connections in the village, offered to be responsible for the letters and we drove away with the six in our clutches.

The next morning I rushed to the British Museum to check the G. B. Hill edition of Johnson's letters, and R. W. Chapman's lists of others he had found. Nothing there to a Mrs. Way! But I did find her name mentioned in a letter of Johnson's to Mrs. Thrale. Quickly, Mr. Gaster had photostats of the letters made, and a set was sent to R. W. Chapman in Oxford, whose great three-volume edition of Johnson's letters was in page proof. Back came word that these were obviously genuine manuscripts, and that he thought he could slip them into an appendix, although it would be a narrow squeeze. And so the letters to Mrs. Way were added to the Johnsonian canon, because of a casual glance of an amused visitor at a Bucks village celebration.[10]

One must admit that in some cases chance merely provides what could have been secured in other ways, though with more trouble. A cynical observer might wonder why Anna Kitchel had not earlier traced Lewes's granddaughters. Even though their names were different, surely it might have been possible to discover them through reading wills. Her experience on top of the London bus could be interpreted as an example of luck rescuing a researcher from failure due to the inadequacy of her own investigations.

Of course, the process can also work in reverse. There are many tales of bad luck thwarting a biographer. In a later chapter I will recount an instance of the casual destruction of records just before the biographer came on the scene. There the timing was unfortunate. With all the best planning possible, there are always accidental elements over which the biographer has no control. But at least he can place himself at the right spot. As samples of just how this can work let me recount various adventures I had many years ago. If luck, in each case, was the determining factor, I was at least part detective, following definite clues. Here is the first tale.

2. The Vague Footnote ৶ Nothing, it might seem, could be less romantic and thrilling than a footnote. Yet one short comment at the bottom of a page set me off on a remarkable set of adventures. It came about this way.

Years ago, through reading A. Edward Newton's delightful *Amenities of Book Collecting*, I became interested in Dr. Johnson's friend Mrs. Thrale. Newton insisted that she had been unfairly treated by history. After the death of Thrale, her sensational marriage in 1784 to an Italian music master had horrified London society, and had saddened Johnson's last months. All this was hard to forgive. But what was even more responsible for her continuing unfortunate reputation was Boswell's jealousy as a rival biographer of Johnson and his constant harping on her inaccuracy and surface flippancy. It was time, Newton insisted, that she be reassessed.

What had the lady really been like? Was she essentially selfish and heartless, brazen and ostentatious, as the traditional account would have it? Or did she truly deserve Johnson's long devotion? Had her apparent callousness and trivial chatter been merely a defense against harsh masculine criticism? The more I thought about the problem, the more curious I became, and in a desultory way I began collecting books about her. One that I stumbled on was *Dr. Johnson and Mrs. Thrale,* by an eccentric book collector and journalist named A. M. Broadley. Published in 1910, it proved to be a strange mélange, which printed for the first time Mrs. Thrale's journal of her trip to Wales with Dr. Johnson in 1774, as well as a number of other hitherto unprinted pieces. A pleasant unpretentious book, it was filled with out-of-the-way information. But what caught my attention was a footnote on page 59, where among other remarks, Broadley wrote: "There are two important collections of Piozzi letters in Wales which still await an editor. In the one case her correspondent was her old coachman Jacob, to whom she wrote in a familiar, gossipy vein. The second collection is bound up in no less than sixteen volumes, and are addressed to a lifelong friend and neighbour." What was fascinating and maddening about the note was its vagueness. Where were the collections?—in Wales!

To whom were the letters written? No last names given! Obviously Broadley wished to brag about his superior knowledge, but did not want any rival collector exploiting his discovery. That was in 1910. By 1934, when I chanced on the footnote, nothing was changed. The letters were still not in print, and no later book even mentioned their existence.

Once my curiosity was aroused, it was natural to wonder what was in those two correspondences. Obviously the first step must be to try to get in touch with Broadley or his heirs. But I soon found that Broadley had died just after the First World War, leaving no family. His publishers knew nothing about what had happened to his papers. Nor did any of the principal Johnsonian scholars in the United States or Great Britain. I received courteous replies to my inquiries, but no specific information. The trail seemed to have come to an end—unless I could somehow get to Wales myself.

The lively Hester Thrale-Piozzi had become by this time the topic for my Ph.D. dissertation at Columbia University. Fortunately in the spring of 1935 I was awarded a traveling fellowship for a year abroad to search for all the evidence I could find, and in June I crossed the Atlantic on the first leg of the great adventure. Accompanying me for the summer months was a young cousin, Bob Orr, a senior at Hotchkiss School, eager for anything, whether it might be golf on the windswept links at Harlech, an evening of darts in a snug little pub, or turning up a cache of eighteenth-century letters. Since everything was equally exciting, he was a perfect traveling companion. After purchasing new bicycles in London, we prepared to head west.

But first it seemed advisable to exhaust all the ordinary sources of information. Of course, we went to Oxford to see my friend Jim Osborn, and to meet Dr. R. W. Chapman and Dr. L. F. Powell, the eminent Johnsonian editors. Then I planned to visit the National Library of Wales at Aberystwyth, and to interview the Professor of English Literature at the University of North Wales in Bangor.

The only specific information I garnered in Oxford was the name of the people who now lived in Mrs. Piozzi's old home in

Flintshire. All along I had suspected that my trail would eventually lead to the area around Brynbella, the Italian villa which the Piozzis had built in the early 1790's on an eminence overlooking the Vale of Clwyd. Here it was that Mrs. Piozzi had devotedly nursed her ailing second husband through his last painful years. It seemed logical to suppose that Broadley's "somewhere in Wales" had actually not been quite so vague as it sounded. The chances were that the letters were in the vicinity of Mrs. Piozzi's house, though where was still a mystery, for I knew that all of her relations were gone. Naturally I had planned to concentrate my search in this area of North Wales, and I was glad to have the names of the present occupants of the house, a Mr. and Mrs. Herbert Evans.

But with this information came news that was a bit disturbing. Mrs. Evans, in letters to Dr. Powell, had incidentally mentioned having seen the ghost of Mrs. Piozzi on a number of occasions. Indeed, she insisted that the spirit of Johnson's friend still haunted the house and gardens. When Dr. Powell passed on this nugget of news, his eyes gleamed. He chuckled and shook his head, as he imagined my interview with the present mistress of Brynbella, evidently picturing me at a Flintshire séance, calling up the spirit of the long-departed Mrs. Piozzi, to ask her personally about the whereabouts of her letters.

The people at the National Library of Wales were friendly and helpful, but had no special knowledge of Piozzian manuscripts. Similarly, at the University of North Wales, the professor who held the chair in English literature knew nothing of any manuscript collections in the neighborhood. When shown Broadley's footnote, all he could do was shrug his shoulders and confess ignorance. But he could tell me the names of two families in Flintshire who certainly went back to the eighteenth century—the Mainwarings and the Pennants. Whether or not they had old manuscripts he had no idea, but at least they might have. And that was as far as I could get through official sources.

And so one sultry July afternoon my cousin and I cycled into St. Asaph, hot and thirsty, a few more miles to go to Denbigh, which we had planned as our center of operations. We had expected to spend only a short time in St. Asaph, just enough for a glimpse of the small cathedral and a drink, but fate had ordained otherwise. We never did cycle down the smooth road from St. Asaph to Denbigh. Once we were inside the cathedral doors we were in the hands of some irresistible force which carried us from one adventure to another.

The trigger which set us off was my decision to talk to everyone I met, outlining my problem. Obviously most of the people would think I was a bit touched, but then, an American would be expected to be different. And what did it matter if they thought me crazy? I would never see any of them again. If one in a hundred had ever heard of Mrs. Piozzi, he might have valuable information, and nothing else mattered.

Strolling into the cathedral, I saw my first opportunity to put my theory into practice. Near the chancel was a youngish clergyman, talking to the verger. When there was a lull in the conversation, I stepped up, introduced myself as an American scholar searching for manuscripts of an eighteenth-century lady who had once lived in the neighborhood of St. Asaph. The name Hester Lynch Piozzi brought only a blank stare, but that of Dr. Johnson was another matter. He had heard of the Doctor and had a copy of Boswell on his shelves. To be sure, he had not opened it for years. He was greatly surprised that Johnson's friend Mrs. Thrale had had any connection with Flintshire. But, his interest aroused, he asked the two of us to come to the vicarage for a cup of tea. Hot, dusty, and thirsty as we were, we did not hesitate a moment. Soon we were trundling our bikes down the hill to his modest house about a quarter of a mile away.

The plates of buttered scones and cups of ruddy tea soon revived our spirts, and we found our hosts wholly delightful. There was never a more friendly couple than John Alan Thomas and his wife. Welsh to the core, he was completely bilingual. Stocky, with a red face and benevolent smile, he was simple and lovable. His devoted wife had indefinable charm. As we chatted away, the vicar asked us where we expected to spend the night. On our admission that we had no specific reservations, they insisted that we stay with them for as long as we were in the vicinity. Of course, we allowed ourselves to be persuaded. That one remark in the cathedral gave us a base of operations for our whole stay in Flintshire.

The next morning the vicar took me up to the Cathedral to be introduced to the Dean, who obligingly offered to write letters of introduction to any local people I might name. He, too, was as friendly as could be, though he knew nothing about Mrs. Piozzi and her association with Flintshire.

The day was clear and sunny, and the vicar in an infectious, holiday mood. With no official duties until a service at five, he offered to drive us in his tiny Austin up into the mountains to see the scenery at Betws-y-coed, which we had missed as we came around on our bicycles. Since we had no specific plans, we readily fell in with his suggestion. But on the way I asked if we could stop at Denbigh where we were expecting letters. I had written to Mrs. Herbert Evans, the lady who lived at Brynbella, asking her to reply poste restante at Denbigh, indicating whether we could call to see the house. Perhaps there had been insufficient time for an answer, but I was eager to see.

At the Denbigh Post Office there was nothing for me, but Bob had a stack of letters from his family. While I idly waited as he dashed off an answer, a well-dressed lady of about sixty came into the office and asked the clerk if she could leave a letter for a Mr. Clifford, who would call later. I could hardly believe my ears. At once I introduced myself to Mrs. Evans and she said she would be very happy to show me through her house, though she knew very little about its past history. Then, firmly, she set that afternoon as a convenient time. Under the circumstances I had no wish to suggest an alternative. Thus we never did see Betws-y-coed. The chain of coincidence was already in control. Instead of heading for the mountains, the vicar showed us something of the neighborhood and then drove us to Brynbella about the middle of the afternoon.

Mrs. Evans at once made clear that her knowledge of Mrs. Piozzi was rudimentary, though since childhood she had been aware of the lady's existence through reading Boswell. She herself was not Welsh, and knew very little about this part of the country. Brought up in an army family, she had lived all over the world. She and her second husband, a Liverpool business man, merely rented the place. Even from this casual explanation one could sense her forceful character. Handsome, poised, fluent, she was quite obviously a woman of the world, with grace and an iron will. Could this be the "wild Welsh lady" that Dr. Powell had talked about in Oxford, who saw ghosts and held so obstinately to her strange theories?

As soon as I was able, I showed her Broadley's vague footnote. No, she had no idea of what had been meant. After all, since she had been in the Vale for only two years, she was still something of a stranger in the neighborhood. She could tell me something about the house but nothing about any manuscripts. Then she asked me whether I had any idea at all of what local people might be helpful. I replied that the only names of old families that I had were the Mainwarings and the Pennants. I knew they had some connections with Mrs. Piozzi in the eighteenth century. With this, Mrs. Evans began to laugh.

"Miss Pennant and Miss Mainwaring are coming here after tea this very afternoon," she said. "If you will stay on you can ask them personally what they have." Again the impossible! Of course, we accepted at once, and the kindly vicar went home by himself.

The house, which Mrs. Evans now showed us in detail, was architecturally something of a charming hybrid. Like its name, half Welsh and half southern European, Brynbella was an Italian villa transplanted to British soil. The curving stone façade overlooking the valley was flanked by wings which had been increased in height during the nineteenth century. Inside, the fireplaces and ceilings had been executed by Italian workmen, brought to Wales especially for this purpose, though here, too, there were evidences of Victorian alterations.

The formal gardens were admirably kept, and our guide delighted in showing off her annuals, and in pointing out the high brick walls erected by the Piozzis for the protection of fruit. Our first view from the front of the house, high on the bryn, was breathtaking. We could see across the lovely Vale of Clwyd to the distant mountains, with even a glimpse to the north of the blue sea and the Great Orme. Below us was the stream, meandering through farms and villages. The Piozzis had chosen a perfect spot for their home. I remembered so well the story of that choice—how one day as their coach toiled along the road at the top of the bryn, they had come to a place where there was a superb view to the west and north. Here, she had said, we will build our new house. And so she did.

Extending below the house were two levels of smooth lawn, the lower set up for croquet. Proudly Mrs. Evans pointed out the eighteenth-century device, the "Ha! Ha!"—the sunken fence which kept cattle off the lawn but remained invisible to viewers from the house.

At four-thirty we were called in for tea. Our talk, of course, was mostly about Mrs. Piozzi. Once in a slight lull in the conversation, Mrs. Evans calmly remarked:

"I know exactly what Mrs. Piozzi looked like because I have seen her twice."

Here was the first confirmation of the strange story I had heard in Oxford.

"Where did you see her?"

"At the end of a walk in the garden," she went on. "It was April 12 of the first year we were in the house. I was walking in the garden about dusk, when suddenly I saw someone on the other side—a little lady, inconspicuously dressed in eighteenth-century style, with an Italian shawl thrown over her shoulders. Her expression showed deep grief. At once I recognized her as Mrs. Piozzi from her resemblance to her portraits."

"What happened then?" I asked.

"When I started in her direction she suddenly disappeared."

"But you said you had seen her twice."

"Yes, exactly a year later, on April 12 of this year. The same day! There she was again, and wearing exactly the same clothes. What do you think happened in her life on this particular day of the year?"

I had no answer ready. Why, indeed, the 12th of April? The date meant nothing at all to me. It corresponded with no crucial period in her life that I knew about. I had to admit to being in a complete quandary. Airily Mrs. Evans dismissed the topic. "Oh, you will find that out for me some time." And then she went on to chat about the design of the Italian mantelpiece.

After tea, Mrs. Evans asked us to help her set up a ping-pong table on the lawn before the house. She was a great enthusiast, but had found no one in the Vale of Clwyd who could keep up with her fast game. It was dreadfully disappointing! Though she was trying to teach some of the local ladies, they were still rank beginners. When Bob admitted that he could play a little, she handed him a paddle. It only required a minute for her to see that here was the answer to her prayers. Straight from an American preparatory school, Bob could slash and rally with skill and abandon. Soon he and our hostess were locked in a frantic encounter, oblivious to everything about them. For the first time on home grounds, Mrs. Evans had met her match.

Even when Miss Pennant and Miss Mainwaring arrived, their hostess refused to be budged from the ping-pong table. But this was a perfect arrangement from my point of view, for it left me free to ply these two ladies with questions about Piozzian manuscripts.

Miss Pennant, with large features and graying hair, wearing well-worn tweeds, and obviously an expert horsewoman, soon provided the answer to one of my puzzles. Yes, her brother, who lived nearby at Nantlys, had Mrs. Piozzi's letters to her coachman, Jacob. If I would call there the next afternoon I might have a look at them.

Miss Mainwaring, also in her late fifties, was not the athletic type. Short and rotund, she was jolly and talkative, full of anecdotes about the neighborhood and local families. Being herself related to the Salusburys, she proved a mine of information. Of course, I plied her shamelessly with questions. Though not absolutely certain, she thought that her cousin, Sir Randle Mainwaring, possessed the other collection, reputed to be bound in sixteen volumes. If Bob and I would come to lunch with her tomorrow she would give us lunch on Mrs. Piozzi's plates, and by then she would be able to tell us about the manuscripts. So in a few minutes on the lawn at Brynbella, while a ping-pong ball whisked merrily across a nearby table, I was able to solve the whole mystery of Broadley's footnote. No special skills required, only being at the right spot at the right time! It was almost too easy.

As a matter of fact, the ending did not come quite so speedily, for it turned out that Mr. Pennant was away and Sir Randle Main-waring was ill. But I soon knew where the material was and was promised a sight of it. To look ahead a moment—when I did see what Sir Randle had I was in for even a greater surprise. When I finally visited him at his home at Hafod-y-coed, he spread out on the table over six hundred unpublished letters of Mrs. Piozzi mostly to his great-grandmother, bound in twelve volumes. As I had feared, however, they were all in her late life, long after Johnson had died. Sir Randle sensed my disappointment, and said "You were hoping for something in the Johnson period?" I admitted as much. "Yes, there are so many surviving letters from these years, in the Rylands Library and elsewhere. There is almost an embarrassment of riches. But there just isn't enough about her early married years."

"So you would like to find more evidence about the Thrale period?"—in a teasing tone.

"I would give anything," I blurted out, "for a series of letters in the 1760's and 1770's."

"Would this, then, be of any use to you?" he continued, as his smile broadened. He passed over an old notebook, bound in brown leather.

Here again were pages in the lady's clear, forceful handwriting, but this time it was the dates which caught my eye—1766 on the first page and continuing through the 1770's.

"You must be a magician," I spluttered. "Where, how, when did you get this? I've never even suspected it existed. None of the people who have written about her have ever mentioned this."

"Look it over," he said, "see exactly what it is."

I turned it over in my hand. On the outside was written in large letters the title "Children's Book or Rather Family Book." Inside, the first entry began when Hester Maria, or "Queeney" as Johnson called her, the eldest child, was two years old; and the last recorded the death of her husband Henry Thrale in 1781. In between there were accounts of the births and deaths of her children, descriptions of their illnesses, their accomplishments, of various domestic crises at Southwark and Streatham. Except for some bright sayings of Queeney there were few flashes of Mrs. Thrale's usual humor or caustic wit. This was the moving and pathetic record of a typical eighteenth-century mother—twelve births and eight deaths. A tragic account, when squeezed together into one small book—an agonizing, extremely personal record of symptoms and remedies, of faulty diagnoses by eminent physicians, of buried hopes and lost affections. For mastoid infection two babies were systematically bled to death; for an attack of appendicitis her only son was dipped in water as hot as he could stand, with the result that he was dead in a few hours. Bleedings, emetics, purges—how even four of the children survived is a mystery.

Merely a quick look was enough to show me that this was what I had been desperately hoping to find—something to show the other side of the Mrs. Thrale who appears selfish and callous in Boswell's pages. Here was her tragic inner life as a young matron and mother. This was not the witty hostess, but the distraught human being. And what made the discovery more exciting was the fact that I could see the name "Mr. Johnson" coming in and out of the record. Even with such a hurried look as I had that day, it was clear that here must be the basis for any genuine description of the life of the Thrales and Dr. Johnson for some fifteen years. Yet I had never dreamed of its existence. Only through my following the clue of Broadley's vague footnote concerning other material had I accidentally turned it up. Sir Randle, amused by my excitement, at once offered to send all of his manuscripts over to Oxford for the winter where I could study them at leisure.[1]

Unfortunately, I was due back in London the next day, and thus was forced to rush away leaving Mrs. Evans absorbed in her new acquisitions. But in a few weeks I was back again for my last visit that year to the glorious Vale of Clwyd, and this time I was in no hurry. At long last I could get everything I needed. With the permission of my hosts, I set up my camera in one of the upstairs bedrooms and photographed all the important letters and diary entries. With hundreds of snapshots I could continue to study the evidence even when on the other side of the Atlantic. A few of the precious originals I carried away to show the Oxford Johnsonians.[1]

Almost a year after that exciting day when Bob and I first braved the dangers of a visit to Bach-y-graig, I could write "finis" to one of the most exhausting adventures of my life.

4. The Paralyzed Old Lady ?❧ As every detective

knows, clues keep turning up which are quite unconnected with the main problem, but which eventually lead to others equally important. A stray remark or a seemingly futile suggestion may start one off on a completely new trail. And the scholar soon learns that it is never safe to ignore any possible lead.

At lunch with Miss Susan Mainwaring on that first visit to the Vale of Clwyd I tried to draw her out about her relationship to the Salusburys. While admitting comparative ignorance, she let fall the fact that her older sister, a Mrs. Knollys, who lived near London, was much more interested in family history. I jotted down the name and address in my notebook, and promptly forgot all about it. Not until the following December did I finally get around to following up the suggestion. Then I found that the long delay had almost proved disastrous.[1]

My first advance was a letter explaining my quest and asking for permission to call. Weeks went by and there was no answer. At last through Miss Pennant I heard that Mrs. Knollys had had a stroke and was in a nursing home in South Kensington. That lead, I thought to myself, was now a blind alley.

A few days later, however, there came a note from Mrs. Knollys's daughter, a Mrs. Carroll, acknowledging my letter and giving the same sad news. But, she added, her mother was very eager to see me. Despite the fact that she was partially paralyzed and could not talk clearly, she was determined to tell me something about Mrs. Piozzi. Mrs. Carroll suggested a day for a visit and provided instructions about reaching the nursing home.

The invitation set me in something of a quandary. Naturally I was eager to go, but I really had very little to ask. Why should I trouble the poor old lady? Suppose the excitement of my visit brought on another stroke? How could I justify taking such a risk, merely to satisfy my chance curiosity? It seemed a foolish thing to do. Yet the daughter's note was insistent. Surely she ought to know what her mother could stand.

Mrs. Carroll met me in the parlor of the nursing home and prepared me to some extent for what was to come. Her mother, she said, was not completely paralyzed. She could move her head slightly, and one arm. While not able to talk coherently, she could make noises and some simple words. What was beyond her was pronouncing proper names and descriptive phrases. But they had gradually worked out a means of communication and she thought, even though it might take time, that we could find out what her mother wished to tell us.

We found Mrs. Knollys propped up in her bed, vainly trying to smile a welcome. At a glance I could see that she was an unusual person. Well over eighty, with silvery hair and a benign expression, she easily dominated the room even in her passive condition. The widow of an admiral, she had been socially prominent all her life. She had once been a lady-in-waiting to Queen Victoria. Her mother had been presented to George IV, her daughter to Edward VII, and her granddaughter to George V. Tradition and breeding were evident in her very appearance, her calm pride and air of distinction.

As Mrs. Carroll had explained to me, Mrs. Knollys's mother had been a daughter of Sir John Salusbury, Mrs. Piozzi's adopted son and heir, and she remembered him well. Thus I was now sitting in the same room with someone whose acquaintance went back to people who had actually known my lady. I was only two removes away.

For a while Mrs. Carroll did most of the talking, describing family relationships, filling in details, as her mother nodded and smiled. She was so eager to pass on information to me, and so apologetic over her inability to talk plainly, that it was frustrating for her to have to sit back and let someone else mangle her stories.

One of the things her mother had wished to tell me, so Mrs. Carroll said, was that all of their family papers had been burned in a warehouse fire during the First World War. Nothing of any importance was left to show me. Nor did the Mostyn branch of the family have anything. I might avoid a fruitless search in that direction. No need to hunt for Mrs. Piozzi's letters to her daughter

Cecilia, who had married John Mostyn. About the middle of the nineteenth century members of the Mostyn family searching for some lost documents happened to come across a metal securities box which they at once assumed contained stocks and bonds. Though the key was missing, they finally were able to pry the box open, to find to their disgust that it contained only a great bundle of Mrs. Piozzi's letters. So angry and disappointed were they that they threw the whole lot in the fire.

One message that her mother was anxious to pass on to me, Mrs. Carroll added, she had so far not been able to interpret. It had something to do with a letter which Mrs. Knollys had seen years before, then in the possession of someone else. All that she could tell me was that the letter was very important. Now, however, with my help, she would like to try again.

For the next half hour I participated in one of the strangest colloquies one could imagine. The daughter kept asking an interminable set of questions, and the partly paralyzed mother would answer by nods or half indistinguishable sounds.

"Was it a business letter?"

There was a shake of the head.

"Was it a literary letter?" Another shake.

"Did it have to do with Mrs. Piozzi's literary career?" Still another.

Social gossip, family affairs, politics, travel—on and on went the questions, always with a negative reply.

"Was it a love letter?" Mrs. Carroll finally asked. There was a quick affirmative nod.

"Perhaps a letter of proposal?" An even more vigorous nod of approval.

"To Mrs. Piozzi herself?" I interposed.

Again there was the movement of assent.

"From Piozzi?"

This time the motion of the head was negative.

"From some rejected suitor?"

Another negative.

"From Henry Thrale, her first husband?"

A decided bobbing up and down with noises of pleasure.

Finally we had it—Thrale's letter of proposal to the young Miss Salusbury. Strange that I had never heard of this before. One would expect that such an important letter, even though in private hands, might have been well known.

"Was it a formal letter?" I went on. "That is what he probably would have written. I can't imagine much else from the stolid brewer."

There could be no doubt of the adverse reaction.

So I tried other descriptive phrases—conservative, curt, carefully-worded, flowery. No success.

"Ardent," Mrs. Carroll broke in.

A vigorous nod of assent.

It was hard to believe. An ardent love letter from Henry Thrale! Everything that we knew about his cold, phlegmatic temperament made such a thing incredible. It was well known that his marriage to Hester Lynch Salusbury had been merely one of convenience. What he wanted was the £10,000 dowry offered by her well-to-do uncle. There had never been the slightest suggestion, so far as I knew, of passion about the alliance. He and his bride had never been alone for more than a few moments before their marriage. Surely the old lady must be mistaken.

But I could not let her see my disbelief. No need to hurt her feelings, for she was so pleased with herself at having been able to pass on the information to me. Besides, we still had more to discover.

Again began the long series of questions. First, when had she seen it? That proved relatively easy. By quick elimination we arrived at a period of about forty years earlier. Who had it then? At this point it was necessary to rely wholly on Mrs. Carroll, who patiently named all of her mother's old friends whom she could remember. At last there was a bright nod of assent.

"That lady has been dead for many years," Mrs. Carroll commented. "But I happen to know her son, Major Delmar Morgan.

Would you like to have me find out from him whether he knows anything about this mysterious letter?"

"Please do," I eagerly begged of her. "If there is any way at all of finding out whether the letter still exists and where it is, I should be overjoyed."

It was so agreed.

With that the amazing interview concluded, and expressing profuse thanks I slipped out of the room. As I softly closed the door, the last view I had was of the lovely white-haired old lady, exhausted but triumphant, slumped back on the cushions of her bed.

ફ**

A few weeks later there came a kind note from Major John Delmar Morgan inviting me to tea the following Sunday. No mention was made of the letter or of any manuscripts. But, I reasoned, why should he ask me to call if he knew nothing about the matter?

The Morgans lived in an attractive house in Chelsea, filled with literary and artistic mementos. Mrs. Morgan explained that she had been the daughter of the Victorian poet, Frederick Locker-Lampson, and regaled us through tea with reminiscences of her early days. Whenever I tried to bring the conversation around to Mrs. Piozzi and Thrale's supposed letter of proposal, she would airily reply with some vague remark about getting to that later. Then would follow another amusing anecdote. Kate Greenaway, it turned out, had been an intimate friend of the family, and I was shown many of her original sketches and drawings. As an old man, Tennyson had sometimes visited them. Laughingly Mrs. Morgan recalled the first time the poet, with his great shock of hair, had appeared for dinner, when her younger brother in a loud voice had demanded of his father if this was the new tutor. Of all things Tennyson detested it was remarks of this sort, for his egotism by this time was excessive. Not to be known by everyone was humiliating.

Gaily Mrs. Morgan told other stories about the Laureate, giving excruciatingly funny examples of his eccentricities and pride, all seen from the point of view of a young girl growing up in the late nineteenth century.

An hour or so passed most agreeably, yet with no further mention of the reason for my visit. A few hesitant attempts on my part to change the subject were unavailing. I could not pin them down at all about the Thrale letter. At last I grew desperate.

"Please tell me," I interposed, looking squarely at Major Morgan, "if you know anything about any old manuscripts owned by your mother some forty years ago."

"Oh, yes, she had some things," he replied. "I remember we had them after her death."

"Was there a letter of proposal from Henry Thrale to Miss Salusbury?" With determination I tried my best to draw a direct answer.

"It seems to me," he smiled in a vague manner, "that there was something like that, but, really, how can I remember after all these years."

"You believe you actually had some such letter?" I was implacable.

"Oh, my dear chap," he went on pleasantly, "we've had so many manuscripts. You can't expect me to be certain."

Refusing to give up, I pressed on to the crucial question.

"Can you tell me where your mother's papers are now?"

"I thought we told you that." He smiled again. "We sold them all years ago."

My heart sank, and I am afraid I did not hide my disappointment. Yet I had to go on with one more query.

"Do you mind telling me to whom you sold them?"

"At Sotheby's, of course. They were auctioned off with some other things. We needed the money at the time, and so they had to go."

"When was the sale?"

He struggled hard over that one, wrinkling his forehead in a show of dismay. Again he insisted that he simply could not remember. It had been years ago, of that he was certain.

"Isn't there any way that you can be more precise about the date?" I pleaded. "Surely you can fix it within a few years."

With that the Major and his wife began a valiant attempt to provide an answer. Mrs. Morgan seemed to remember that they had always kept those manuscripts in a closet under the stairs. Not in the present house, of course. They had only lived here for a short time. Now, which house had had that closet under the stairs? Mrs. Morgan thought it was the one they had lived in before the war; the Major was certain it was after the war. It all came down to the fact that they simply could not remember. So, when the digressions began to run away with the original question I was forced to give up.

All that I knew was that shortly before, or shortly after, the First World War the Morgans had sold some manuscripts at Sotheby's. And I had a feeling that the Major's arguments were more conclusive, and that it had been after. With that guess I had to be content.

So we were back again on Tennyson and Locker-Lampson. I had gleaned all that was possible here, and gladly let myself be carried along on the delightful stream of literary reminiscences. Soon I was laughing as heartily as my hostess, everything else forgotten.

ತ⋙

Although not quite certain just what could be gleaned at Sotheby's without more accurate information, I walked down the next afternoon to New Bond Street. I had been to the auction rooms several times before, to watch the sales of rare books, but was unfamiliar with the business offices of the firm. A general query at the door, however, brought me to an agreeable elderly clerk, who listened courteously to my story.

What I wanted to know was whether they had sold some manuscripts for a Major John Delmar Morgan shortly after the war, or perhaps just before it. Was there any way to trace the sale? That would be easy, he replied, since they had ledgers listing all former clients. He left me, and in a few minutes returned with the information that among autograph letters sold on February 3, 1919, there were listed various properties belonging to Major Morgan.

Happily I now had the exact date. Did they have any descriptions of the items sold? No, he replied, but I would find a marked copy of the same catalogue in the British Museum, where there was a complete set of earlier numbers. I hurried back to Great Russell Street, and put in a request for the issue that I wished to see. The trail was beginning to get warm.

As I sat waiting in the general reading room, I kept wondering what the catalogue would show. Could it be possible that there really was a letter of proposal from Thrale? Or was that merely a slip of memory on the part of the aging Mrs. Knollys? Perhaps she had mistaken the name. The letter she had seen might well have been to someone else. Or it might even have been written by another person. I was pretty certain that there must be something wrong about the description.

An hour passed, and my curiosity was consuming. Would the catalogue never come? Vainly I tried to concentrate on other books piled on my desk. Finally it arrived, and I skimmed through the pages until I came to a series of items marked "The Property of Major John Delmar Morgan." My eyes were riveted on lot 382. "A letter of proposal to Miss Salusbury and Mrs. Salusbury from Henry Thrale." It was hard to believe, yet there it was. I read the description over again. The lovely old lady had been vindicated, and all my doubts unwarranted.

Yet I was still puzzled. Why had the Johnson enthusiasts, why had A. Edward Newton never mentioned this obviously important letter? Why had I never heard of it before? Apparently in 1919 it had come briefly to the surface and then disappeared, leaving not so much as a ripple. Strange! and tantalizing!

Where was it now? Though I knew it existed, the major problem remained. How trace its present whereabouts? In the margins of the British Museum copy of the catalogue were pencil notations giving the names of purchasers for each item. Opposite No. 382

was written "Stevens and Brown," a well known London rare book dealer. Without delay I dashed off to their premises.

Hastily I asked my question: "Do you keep any specific records of sales of manuscripts? Is it possible, for example, to tell what happened to an autograph letter which you bought at Sotheby's in 1919?"

The clerk shook his head. "That would depend on how valuable the manuscript was. It might be possible to trace some outstanding item. But generally letters are bought and sold and no permanent record kept."

My face fell. I had somehow hoped there might be something to consult. This was a bitter disappointment. Just the same, I went on to explain about my present search. The clerk examined my notes about the Thrale letter, and listened sympathetically to my story.

"I'm sorry," he said, "I wish we could help you, but I'm certain that we have no way of telling what happened to that piece." Then he added, "But I'll ask one of the partners. There's just a chance that he might know."

Again a complete blank. He, too, was courteous and kindly, but could add nothing.

"How could we remember every autograph that passes through our hands?" He smiled wryly. "And if we tried to keep records, we would soon have no room for our stock. You can see for yourself how impossible it would be. Someone may have come into our shop, chanced to see the letter you are interested in, paid for it in currency, and then walked off with it under his arm, and we would never have been aware of his name. Or it might have been sent by mail to any part of the world. There is no way of telling."

There was a finality about his explanation, which left little cause for optimism. The trail had evidently come to an abrupt end. To be sure, it was something to know that the letter actually existed. But where?

Nevertheless, I refused to give up. "I know this may be something you cannot answer," I began hesitantly, "but in 1919 what important clients of yours might have been buying Johnsonian items? Could you give me any hints at all?"

He smiled. "Back in those years almost everything was going over to the United States. The chances are strong that the letter is owned by one of your countrymen."

"Which American collectors did you chiefly supply?" I persisted.

"Oh, in those days Mr. R. B. Adam of Buffalo was buying anything connected with Johnson. My guess is that it went to him."

"But Adam in 1929 printed a sumptuous four-volume catalogue of his entire collection," I said, "and there is no mention of this letter. If he bought it in 1919 it would certainly have been included. I know those volumes almost by heart, and there is no mention of any Thrale letter such as this."

"Well," said the partner, "I'm very sorry, but his is the only name I can suggest. I'm afraid we can give you no other help than that."

As I walked out of the door at Stevens and Brown, I could see little to hope for. Here was I in England and possibly somewhere in America was the letter I wanted to see. In San Francisco, or Boston, or Houston, Texas (How could I tell where?) it was probably lying unread in some autograph collector's album. There was obviously nothing to do but forget about the whole affair. This was evidently fated to be one of my failures. Reluctantly I threw myself into other concerns.

ॐ

For almost a year I did nothing more about the lost letter. But I could never quite forget. Then, back in the United States, trying to complete the first draft of my life of Mrs. Piozzi, I decided to make one last effort. This was one piece I desperately needed for my book. Perhaps Mr. R. B. Adam might know something. At least there would be no harm in asking.

Accordingly, I wrote to him about my search, how I had first heard of the letter, and about my subsequent disappointment. Was it possible that he owned the letter, even though not listed in his valuable great printed catalogue? Or did he by chance know the present owner? I was so eager to find out what it was like.

By return mail came an answer. Yes, he had Thrale's proposal to Miss Salusbury. He couldn't imagine how it happened to have been left out of his catalogue. Purely an oversight! If I would come to Buffalo some time he would be glad to show me the letter, as well as other rarities in his collection.

A few months later I did go to Buffalo and was hospitably taken by Mr. Adam into his handsome library. The first thing he brought out to me was a small single sheet of paper, still crisp and well preserved, with only slightly faded handwriting. This time the trail had really ended—and with success. There in my hands was the very letter which Mrs. Knollys had tried so valiantly to describe for me in that nursing home in South Kensington. With mounting excitement I slowly read the words the brewer had penned almost 175 years before:

Mr. Thrale presents His most respectfull compliments to Mrs. & Miss Salusbury & wishes to God He could have communicated His Sentiments to them last night, which is absolutely impossible for Him to do to any other Person breathing: He therefore most ardently begs to see Them at any Hour this afternoon, & He will at all Events immediately enter upon this very interesting Subject, & when once begun, there is no Danger of His wandering upon any other: in short, see them, He must, for He assures them, with the greatest Truth & Sincerity, that They have murder'd Peace and Happiness at Home.
June 28, 1763

Henry Thrale[2]

Ardent? Yes, certainly. A letter of proposal? Perhaps, though that is not so certain. Since the marriage came only a few months later, it was a good guess. In any event, for any casual observer there was enough to justify Mrs. Knollys's description. She had been correct in almost every particular.

Yet it seemed to me that I could detect a kind of false, or at least simulated, passion in the phraseology. This was not quite the way someone genuinely in love would write to his beloved. And what attraction there was appeared to be equally distributed between mother and daughter. The more I studied the wording, the more it corresponded to what might have been expected from Thrale. He had to present himself as passionate, but his heart was not in the attempt. Basically, then, both the characterization by the paralyzed old lady and my own skepticism had been right. It was the kind of message into which one might read almost any kind of interpretation. But there could be no doubt of one thing: for a biographer it was the most valuable kind of evidence.

5. A Few Other Cases ✌ Sometimes, of course, being on the spot is practically impossible, and then one's luck may depend on persistent writing of letters. Consider the case of the Campbell diary.

Readers of Boswell may remember that on Wednesday, April 5, 1775, Boswell dined at the Dillys' with Johnson. Another of the company was Dr. Thomas Campbell, "an Irish Clergyman, whom I took the liberty of inviting to Mr. Dilly's table, having seen him at Mr. Thrale's, and been told that he had come to England chiefly with a view to see Dr. Johnson, for whom he entertained the highest veneration."[1] Again on the 8th the three men were together at the Thrales' and on the 10th at General Oglethorpe's. For these occasions Boswell supplied interesting accounts of Johnson's conversation. He surely had no suspicion that Campbell was also keeping a journal and jotting down some of the remarks. Boswell never saw Campbell again, and the Irish clergyman remained for him only a casual acquaintance who had impressed him by his affability and his desire to meet the great Rambler.

For students of the Johnson circle Campbell does have one other claim to remembrance. Years later he projected a life of his compatriot Oliver Goldsmith and did collect some material, though the work was far from completed at the time of his death in 1795, the same year as Boswell's. Eventually Bishop Percy used some of Campbell's materials, but his contribution as a biographer was negligible.[2] Thus the Irish Dr. Campbell, for most readers in the early nineteenth century, was merely a name in a famous book.

Then a strange thing happened on the other side of the globe. In the early 1850's, when straightening up the Supreme Court Room in Sydney, New South Wales, an old press was moved and there hidden behind it was a small pocket book filled with jottings from the eighteenth century. Although it carried no name, once it was carefully examined and comparison made with Boswell's *Life of Johnson* there could be no doubt that it had belonged to Dr. Thomas Campbell. With some omissions, the manuscript was printed in Sydney in 1854,[3] with an Introduction and some notes by

Samuel Raymond, Prothonotary of the Supreme Court of New South Wales. Raymond confessed that he had no knowledge of how the diary had reached the Antipodes, or why it should have turned up where it did, but he thought the old notes of sufficient interest to warrant publication. As might have been expected, this provincial publication stirred up slight interest.

A few years later, perhaps with the idea of attempting to gain some publicity, Raymond sent a copy to Lord Macaulay, who, on May 21, 1859, wrote in his diary of receiving the "curious little pamphlet," and added: "It by no means gives the notion of a blind fanatical worshipper of Johnson, as I had supposed Campbell to be from Boswell's narrative. There are some odd things as coming from a clergyman; and some passages still more indecorous have been omitted."[4] Macaulay had no doubt of the authenticity of the diary. From internal evidence alone this seemed quite clear, and when he found, by searching through Nichols's *Illustrations*, that Campbell's oldest nephew had emigrated to Sydney in 1810, the matter appeared settled. Macaulay passed the little volume around among his friends, one of whom was Henry Reeve, editor of the *Edinburgh Review*. After vainly attempting to get Macaulay to review the diary in his journal, Reeve published a long account in the issue of October, 1859. This brought Campbell's diary to the attention of the general reading public, but apparently there was no serious attempt at that time to republish it in England.

Not all English readers were so favorably impressed as Macaulay. Some found Campbell's notes unimportant, and even doubted their authenticity. In 1882 Benjamin Jowett, the great Oxford scholar, wrote about the diary: "It contains accounts of Conversations with Johnson—which I believe to be forgeries, though I remember Lord Macaulay reproving me for doubting them."[5] He, and others like him, thought the whole thing sounded too pat—it "agreed too much with Boswell."—as if someone wishing to perpetrate a hoax had started with Boswell's accounts in the *Life* and fabricated the rest. This, they concluded, was just another rather crude literary forgery. Moreover, when later attempts to check the text with the original manuscript proved unsuccessful, since the diary could not be found, this fact merely increased the uneasiness of serious scholars.

Mrs. Robina Napier, to be sure, in her volume of supplementary *Johnsoniana* in 1884 did reprint Raymond's text with a few further omissions, and G. B. Hill included a few extracts in his *Johnsonian Miscellanies* in 1897, though with some obvious reluctance. Thus scholars continued to be divided both as to the value of the diary and its authenticity. In the 1920's S. C. Roberts of the Cambridge University Press thought of bringing out a new edition, but soon saw that the Raymond text was unreliable. Obviously nothing could be done until it was possible to consult the original manuscript. Unfortunately, when Roberts wrote to Sydney he was told that the diary had completely disappeared. No one living had ever seen it, and nobody knew where it could be. There the matter rested. When I began my work on Mrs. Thrale-Piozzi in the early 1930's I was told that the manuscript was irretrievably lost, and had possibly been destroyed.

But I decided to make a determined effort at least to secure all the facts. There must be some way to prove it had once existed. The first step was to secure a copy of Raymond's 1854 edition, for there were no copies to consult in the principal American libraries. After I had written to various booksellers in Sydney, I finally did turn up a copy in New South Wales, which I was able to purchase at a very reasonable cost. But none of the dealers with whom I corresponded could give me any help on the major problem of finding the original manuscript. Obviously the next step was to write to the librarians of all the major institutions in New South Wales. At the same time, I tried to find the names of any collectors who might be living in the neighborhood, including any descendants of Raymond or of the Campbells.

One of the librarians who responded to my plea was Miss Ida Leeson of the Mitchell Library in Sydney. She sent me everything she could uncover; she searched her own library, and consulted other local authorities. But, alas, the reports continued to be negative. I was beginning to fear that the search was really hopeless, and was considering, as a last resort, inserting various queries in the Australian newspapers, hoping that some clue might turn up, when suddenly came a break. In July, 1934, I received a long apologetic letter from Miss Leeson with the startling news that she had discovered the manuscript in a drawer in her own library, where it must have been sitting uncatalogued for many years, while Jowett and Hill and the other scholars had been kept wondering and arguing. She added that it was certainly genuine and later on she would arrange to send me photostats.

Gradually, too, we were able to piece together what had happened. Since Dr. Campbell had had no children, at his death everything he owned was inherited by his nephews. The eldest, John Thomas Campbell, when he settled in New South Wales fifteen years after his uncle's death, evidently took the diary with him. In 1821 he became Sheriff and Provost Marshall of the Supreme Court in Sydney, and it was in his former office that the manuscript had been discovered. The provenance was thus clear. After publishing what had been found in 1854, Raymond presented the diary to the Australian Library, and later it had been transferred to the newly formed Mitchell Library. But in those early days library listings were at best hit or miss, and the manuscript never was entered in the general catalogue. Thus it was quickly forgotten, and later librarians had no idea of its presence in their building.

Is there something to be learned from this story? Perhaps only that even fine libraries sometimes do not know about all of their treasures. A simple search through modern catalogue files may not be enough. The next question might be—was it worth all that trouble? The answer is a resounding "Yes." Not only is it reassuring for us to know that the diary is genuine, but also it is important to see just what was left out of that first mid-nineteenth-century edition. Not that the censored passages add much to our knowledge of Johnson and his circle! The one sensational anecdote which Campbell recorded concerning Johnson's reputed reply to the question of what is the greatest pleasure—and his use of a four letter word in his answer—came second-hand through Garrick, and may very well represent a dramatic embellishment. Nevertheless, it is valuable to know that stories like this were being passed around among his friends. And the importance of the diary in checking Boswell's reporting of Johnson's conversation should not be overlooked. We will have more to say about that in the next chapter.

If the recounting of dramatic discoveries such as those I have been describing makes it sound as if the life of the biographical researcher is all sunshine, it should always be remembered that for every Welsh farmhouse or Australian library there are scores of disappointments. The detective tends to brag about his successes. When pressed, he could always tell of one lost clue after another, but it is easier to forget the failures. Even the incredible Boswell discovery is not entirely positive.

Much has been in print about the dramatic story of Boswell's archives—found in Ireland and Scotland—but not so publicized is the fact that one very valuable correspondence has never turned up. If someone had asked Boswell which manuscripts he treasured most, he might well have replied that they were the 120-odd letters he had received from Dr. Johnson. He used them in the *Life*, but often with slight omissions, indicated by asterisks. Where are the originals? Many of us would be curious to see just what Boswell felt he had to leave out. They were not among the mass of papers at Malahide Castle or at Fettercairn House. Could they be hidden in some lawyer's office in Edinburgh? Or elsewhere? This is the sort of tantalizing mystery which haunts the active Johnsonian.

Then there has been a long, fruitless search for the originals of Elizabeth Carter's correspondence with Miss Talbot, mentioned earlier as a sample of nineteenth-century censoring. For all his mangling of the letters, the editor, Montagu Pennington, would hardly have destroyed the manuscripts when he was through. It is unlikely that her letters contained anything which he would have thought shocking. Yet careful study of a long series of wills of Pennington's heirs, together with advertisements in present-day

English newspapers, has not turned up a single clue as to the where-abouts of the manuscripts. My guess is that they are tucked away in some closet of a distant relative, long forgotten and thought to be of no particular interest.

There are, too, the papers of the publisher John Newbery, which were used by the author of *A Bookseller of the Last Century*, which appeared in 1885.[6] As late as 1929, a writer in the *Times Literary Supplement* indicated that the summer before he had been in-dexing Newbery papers for the Public Museum in Reading, yet by the 1960's the material had gone underground again.[7] Included are some receipts signed by Dr. Johnson, and an unpublished auto-biography of Francis Newbery, whom Johnson befriended. More-over, one must remember Newbery's close connection with other major authors of the mid-eighteenth century. Yet Terry Belanger for a year tried in every way to find these papers, consulting wills and interviewing representatives of various branches of the family. At last he did turn up a large cache of Newbery manu-scripts, but none of them was connected with Johnson, Gold-smith, or Christopher Smart. Instead almost all had to do with the patent medicines which the Newberys marketed—including Dr. James's Fever Powders!

ॐ

So far, I have been talking about tracing manuscripts in private hands—those still in the possession of relatives of one's subject, or held by private collectors and public libraries. It must not be for-gotten that there are other places where manuscripts survive, re-positories which until recently have rarely been tapped, but which are now gradually beginning to open up. I refer to the files of doc-tors, lawyers, and bankers. In the past all professional men—doc-tors, lawyers, clergymen, and bankers—have felt that it would be a violation of their trust to allow any outsider to see their profes-sional records. Priests and clergymen rarely, if ever, keep written records of confessions. Doctor's records may be very full, but tend to be highly technical. Complete acceptance of the Hippocratic oath makes most doctors averse to talking to biographers, or to revealing anything about their patients. (I will have more to say about this in the last chapter.) But what about psychiatrists? Will they all feel obliged to destroy their records of interesting cases? Or may some be willing to make them available to posterity? And would the technical records of this kind be of any use to a writer not himself a psychiatrist?

Not quite such an ethical problem are lawyer's records—details of divorce actions, suits over property, all sorts of business negotiations. Obviously they could hardly be made public while suits are in progress, or even soon after. But later? If so, how many years later? Occasionally records of legal cases have come to light which have provided valuable grist to the biographer's mill. A case in point is a legal action involving Henry Fielding as a very young man, described in detail in records at the Public Record Office.[8] The suit had to do with a fierce struggle between father and grandmother over control of the Fielding children. Going right to the heart of the matter, the surviving depositions from various witnesses provide a realistic picture of the living conditions of young Henry. Without them, we would be at a loss to explain much in his character.

Ought we to have some set of rules concerning when private and public records of this sort may safely be made public? Many might agree about public records. Are private lawyer's archives entirely different?[9] In England all wills are made available to the curious at Somerset House, but not many solicitors there would willingly allow anyone to search through their files connected with a recent client. Yet, as the years move on, the pertinence of such papers diminishes. A hundred years after a man and all of his children are dead, how could the release of his financial papers or accounts of his family arguments hurt anyone? Or suppose a man has been dead fifty years and left no descendants whatsoever? There is no one living who has the slightest legal or family relationship to the dead man. May a lawyer reasonably make available to the man's biographer everything he has in his filing cabinets?

This is certainly a vital question. I imagine that each person might approach the matter with mixed feelings. Some, I feel sure, would insist that the lawyer ought to destroy all the evidence or keep it hidden forever. Others might side with me in saying that truth is best served—and the biographer is always searching for truth—when every available fact is considered.

Obviously, the time element is of major importance. It all depends—or so it seems to me—on how old the material is. There can be little argument about recent papers. But when they go back into the eighteenth century, I see few valid arguments for not making them public. Of course, there is always some danger that a character may be blackened—some pious hypocrite proved to have been a lecherous rake, or a decorous maiden lady shown to have had an illegitimate child. But it must be remembered that in all cases the modern lawyer has the duty to look through the papers he holds before exposing them to the biographer, and he has the right to decide what may or may not be used. He does have the physical control of the material. It must be admitted that all this would mean additional work for the lawyer, and not many are willing to give the necessary time. Yet occasionally a lawyer may agree to open his files to prying biographers. I might describe one instance concerned with my Johnsonian researches.

In the fall of 1952, when I was giving all my time to collecting material for a book on the young Johnson, I stayed in Lichfield, where Johnson had spent his youth. Naturally I looked through all of the official town records, hoping for references to Michael Johnson, Sam's bookseller father, who had during his long life been Mayor and Sheriff, as well as holding other offices. And I became intimate with the local antiquarian, Percy Laithwaite, an elderly schoolteacher. We talked and talked about the possibility of there being other sources of information in Lichfield which we had not yet tapped. I asked whether there were any firms going back to the early eighteenth century. He said that there was the law firm of Hinckley, Birch and Crarer in Bird Street, which had been functioning for a long time. Happily he knew a younger member of the firm who might be receptive to our inquiry, and he would talk to him. After some negotiations—obviously such a request was unheard of in the Midlands—we were told that the firm did have a storeroom attached to their offices, where they had all their old case records going back to the seventeenth century. The dust there, he said, must be half an inch thick, for they practically never tried to get anything out. These records were unsorted and uncatalogued, and thus were practically useless. But if I really wanted to see what was there, I would be allowed in, though it was so dirty that I must certainly ruin my clothes. And there it was. It did seem a challenge worth taking, and so I went to a nearby clothing store, where I bought some coveralls. With these for protection, I began the long process of examining the hundreds of dusty packages lining the shelves in the storeroom. Dates and a few names usually provided enough to eliminate most of the cases at once. Others had to be opened and examined. For two days I struggled on, not finding anything connected with the Johnson family. Naturally I was a bit depressed, and ready to give up. Only the very top shelf remained and to get up to that would require borrowing a stepladder. It hardly seemed worthwhile. But I knew that if I did not complete the job I would always wonder what was on that shelf. Reluctantly I finally found a ladder, and pulled down the few packages which were there. Suddenly on one of the bundles I saw a name I recognized—Walmesley. Hurriedly I pulled it open, and there were drafts of letters, documents, etc., all having to do with Gilbert Walmesley, who had been young Sam Johnson's chief patron and supporter. The material thus allowed me to give a much fuller and more revealing portrait of Walmesley in my book than I had ever thought possible. Covered with grime, I was one of the happiest men in all Staffordshire that October day.

For the most part, bankers are just as chary as lawyers of making available to scholars their ancient financial records. Certainly they have just as much right to protect their records, particularly when members of the family are still alive and active. But what of eighteenth-century persons who have left no direct heirs? Do they have to be protected from curious biographers? Again there is sure to be a sharp divergence of opinion. A more practical question might be—where are the banking ledgers and how can they be used? None of the twentieth-century handbooks on historical research give any practical advice. Until very recently no one has even had a suspicion that they might be consulted. As a matter of fact, it is only since the last war that in England some breakthrough has been made. Now a new generation of bank managers, with more genuine interest in history, and more commitment to society in general, has begun the search for old records in their vaults, and has set up ways of consulting them.

I cannot here go into all the ramifications of this approach, but it may be enough to say that bank records may well be the most exciting new source of information for biographers and historians working on eighteenth-century subjects. Merely as a sample, let me cite the work of Geoffrey Beard, a young British art historian, who is now the greatest living authority on plasterwork and interior decoration in famous British country houses. Who were the unnamed artisans who produced the superb walls and ceilings we admire so much? Geoffrey Beard now knows, for he has found in surviving bank records lists of payments by the wealthy owners to the craftsmen. Beard can now tell us, from the dated lists of payments, exactly when the work was done and who received payment. In other words, he can now document accurately, rather than from vague hearsay and guesswork, the steady development of many of the best-known great houses in England.[10]

It was Geoffrey Beard who first alerted me to the possibility of looking at banking records in my own research. Of course, I knew that Samuel Johnson had never been rich enough to keep up a bank account. What money he gradually accumulated in later years, after he had a pension, he allowed his friends—Henry Thrale and William Strahan—to handle for him. But the publishers and booksellers who hired him to write must themselves have had accounts. What might these show about payments to Johnson? If I could find the financial records of Cave, of Dodsley, of Tonson the younger, of Payne, might there not be some revealing payments listed?

For example, we know from a receipt in the Lichfield Birthplace Museum that on February 13, 1758, Johnson received from Tonson £40, which happily rescued Johnson from a sponging house where he had been taken following arrest for debt. The question was whether the payment was connected with the Shakespeare edition. Were there other payments? Obviously I wanted to know. Geoffrey Beard had told me that he believed he had seen the name Tonson in the ledgers of Gosling's Branch of Barclay's Bank in Fleet Street. He suggested that I have a look there. But it was not as easy as that. First I had to convince the bank that I was a reliable person, as well as a thorough scholar. So I began to collect an impressive lot of backers, including Sir William Haley, editor of the London *Times*. Amusingly enough, what finally did the trick was my casual mention that for details about my life they might consult *Who's Who*. The fact that I was there they took as sufficient recommendation, and Mr. Cattell, the local manager, became most helpful and co-operative. We set a date, and when I arrived at the bank one morning in early May, 1966, I was escorted down to a lower floor, deep underground, where I was seated at a bare table. My guide then brought in on a cart a number of huge dusty ledgers, very thick and very heavy. Then he stood and watched me as I worked. Indeed, someone had his eye on me every moment I was in the bank. What they suspected I might do with those huge ledgers I cannot imagine. But they took no chances.

The great ledgers turned out to be records of the mid-eighteenth-century banking firm of Gosling, Bennet and Gosling (later Gosling and Bennet). Each volume contained the accounts of clients, arranged alphabetically (A–L in one volume, and M–Z in another), extending through two or more years. Thus to follow any individual account one had to consult many volumes, and that meant hard work on the part of my attendant, lugging the massive ledgers back and forth from the vaults. It is easy to see why a bank would not want to be overrun with demanding biographers.

I soon saw that the accounts could not be of very great use to me in my present researches, since they represented merely debits and credits for each individual client—that is, deposits and expenditures as they occurred, usually with small items not included. But the chronology was all there—with month and day for each entry. Had I been working on some wealthy man who was receiving and paying out large sums of money the evidence might have been very valuable. For the kind of small sums which Johnson received for his weekly work, it was unlikely that the details would show up here.

Of course, I looked first at the account of the younger Jacob Tonson (the elder's account was not there) for February, 1758, hoping at least to find some record of that payment. Alas! no Johnson was listed during this period. But on February 13, there did appear the entry—"To Mr. Strahan 40/–/–." It was quite clear now what had happened. In his emergency Johnson had called on Strahan, his close friend, who acted as intermediary in securing the money from Tonson. Strahan had then paid Johnson's debts, and released him from the sponging house. Thus the ledger entry did help to straighten out that little affair. But unfortunately the search through other years and other accounts did nothing more to aid me in my researches. Although there were many references to a "Mr. Johnson," they were all obviously to other people, principally to Job Johnson, the bookseller. In the end, then, the net gain for all my labors was one possible sentence for my book, merely pointing out the help of Strahan in this emergency.

But to think of the whole affair as a waste of time would be a mistake. Even though I would be the first to admit that from one point of view the search had been a failure, from another it was a huge success. I did turn up a mass of important evidence for other scholars. Here in detail were Samuel Richardson's financial dealings, and those of Edward Young, author of *Night Thoughts*, and of the Herveys—also a variety of publishers—Lintot, Rivington, Osborne. The very next day I was able to pass on word of my find to Henry Pettit in the British Museum, who delightedly told me that in

Young's later letters, which he was editing, there were frequent references to money matters. This would allow him to annotate the correspondence much more fully. I immediately got off a letter to Eaves and Kimpel, the Richardsonians at Arkansas. They were able subsequently to see the ledgers and glean important facts relating to their own problems. Thus from the broader point of view the search has been of major importance to eighteenth-century scholarship, and since I believe so thoroughly in the importance of cooperative scholarship, I do consider my search through the Gosling bank ledgers well worthwhile.

Furthermore, the whole experience taught me much about what might conceivably be found in old banking records. I still hope somewhere to find the accounts of the publishers I am most interested in. There are four other banks that I know of whose records go back to the eighteenth century—Childs, Coutts, Drummonds, and Hoare—but apparently none of them has the material I am seeking at present. Most of these banks have hard-working archivists, and fairly efficient catalogues and indexes. General queries will be graciously answered. And there remains the possibility that records of other eighteenth-century banks will turn up. As I suggested earlier, the whole matter of the historical use of old banking records is just in its infancy.

Not all public records have been utilized fully by biographers. A possible deterrent may have been what they are called. Who would think of finding anything interesting in sewer records? Yet the sewer rate books, preserved in the Greater London Council Record Office, in County Hall, London, do contain very useful information. The rate collectors went down the street house by house, collecting from the occupants, rather than the owners, and often entered notations like "Removed last month," which may be much more precise than leases. But even more important, from these records one can discover who were the neighbors, what kind of people lived on the same block.[11] A researcher can never be sure where valuable information will turn up.

Once all this mass of information is found, then the biographer has to decide what to do with it. It is all very well, I can imagine some readers saying, to keep insisting on the value of "outside" research, but the main job of the biographer has not been touched. In what follows I will discuss some of the problems connected with the handling of evidence.

Part Two
Putting the Pieces Together

6. Testing Authenticity

One of the chief tasks facing a biographer is evaluating the reliability of the facts he has assembled. Although he may have collected masses of detailed information, if much of it is wrong or even partly biased, then the labor has been largely wasted. Thus before he makes any choice of what to quote, or how to put it into smooth narrative form, he must have winnowed out the chaff. Even if this is a long, tedious process, it has to be done.

But how can a serious researcher differentiate what is to be believed from what is incorrect? Are there any accepted rules for making the selection?[1] The customary answer is to insist that it is all a matter of personal veracity. Some people try to tell the truth; others do not. But is it as simple as that? In my own experience all such generalizations turn out to be delusions. Each decision has its own subtle intricacy.

One keeps asking how authentic is this anecdote, or that, and whether there is any justification for such stories as X tells. How dependable is X? Can we ever believe him? Or is he capable sometimes of twisting evidence, if it works to his advantage? If so, how can one be certain just when this occurs? Is there any way to tell what is peripheral embellishment, and what the basic point of an anecdote? And there are scores of similar questions.

The necessity for rigorous skepticism is continually to be emphasized. If a biographer starts with the assumption that because a well-known respected citizen makes a certain statement it must inevitably be true, there is sure to be trouble ahead. Often the strangest things happen to facts, even in the hands of the most well-meaning persons. As I shall document fully in a moment, truth can get distorted in the subtlest of ways, and it is the duty of any writer of a life to subject each anecdote to severe analysis. Sometimes, to be sure, there is no way to check the truth of an item which came from only one source and with no possibility of substantiation elsewhere. In such instances the item must be considered carefully in the larger context of the work as a whole.

One aspect of the problem of authenticity, which I shall not stress here, is forgery. This would take us into matters of handwriting analysis, watermarks of paper, and other such technical details which I prefer to leave to others. Of course, a biographer must always be alert to the possibility that documents have been fabricated, and in some instances this may be a major difficulty. For the most part there has not been as much chicanery as might be expected, especially in the life records of literary figures. Despite a few noteworthy examples which can be numbered on the fingers of one hand, the amount of forgery, at least in the period I know best, has been slight.

Not long ago there was an attempt to manufacture some letters of the novelist, Tobias Smollett, which just happened to settle various disputed episodes in his life. These were easily exposed by the chief Smollett authorities.[2] With Sterne and with Shelley and a few others there have been some attempts to provide additional letters. It was so easy and financially lucrative to imitate Sterne's style, that a number of writers did so.[3] But with other eighteenth-century authors the amount of successful forgery has been minimal. Indeed, I have often wondered why there have not been more attempts, especially when one considers that only about twenty letters of Henry Fielding have been available, and what collector would not like to own a manuscript by the author of *Tom Jones?* Happily the incipient forgers have found better hunting grounds. I know of few attempts to provide additional letters of Pope or Swift, of Gray or Walpole, Chesterfield or Burke. Where so many have survived and are easily accessible, it would hardly be a very lucrative profession to turn out forged letters of these men or of Mrs. Piozzi or Lady Mary Wortley Montagu.

But if there has been very little criminal forgery of documents concerned with literary figures, a biographer has to be constantly on his guard against certain practices I described in the first chapter—the rewriting of one's own letters and diaries with an eye to eventual publication, and the censorship of later editors. Obviously a scrupulous biographer must learn to be very careful when citing specific details which he knows come from rewritten or carelessly edited material.

In the earlier discussion Alexander Pope was mentioned as an example of someone who rewrote his own letters. The difficulties which such action produces for a modern biographer are illustrated in the case of George Sherburn, who, in 1934, brought out the first really objective and thorough study of the early life of Alexander Pope. He intended to go right on to a second volume describing Pope's later career. But he soon recognized that before he could safely do the job he had first to establish, as best he could, the original text of Pope's correspondence. In other words, he was forced to trace the holograph letters, if they still survived, or dependable copies if they existed. Happily he did find many contemporary copies made for Lord Oxford, and with patient, exhaustive research he turned up large numbers of original manuscripts. The result was that Sherburn's own later career was largely spent in this search. Finally in 1956, twenty-two years after the appearance of his first volume, his five-volume edition of Pope's *Correspondence* was published. At last we have dependable versions of almost 90 percent of Pope's known letters, and they show conclusively that his revisions for publication were largely stylistic, and not vengeful distortions of the truth as had been suspected. Although Sherburn has eradicated one false impression about Pope, it took twenty-two years to do so. And the second volume of his biography was never completed.

Sherburn's is merely one example of how persistence and dedication can bring magnificent results in the establishing of truth. We need many more like him. Where are the originals of the Elizabeth Carter letters, published in a mangled form by her nephew? They must contain a lot about Johnson; the printed versions make this clear. Who will provide us with a reliable text of Anna Seward's letters? Or those of Mrs. Piozzi? When will we be given the original text of Fanny Burney's diary, now safe in the Berg Collection on 42nd Street in New York City? Biographers working in the late eighteenth century badly need texts they can trust. If the evaluation of printed sources can be difficult and exhausting, what can be said about oral tradition? What about the reliability of amusing anecdotes passed on by word of mouth? Here the biographer may be in an even worse position, caught in a quagmire. He may be so firmly caught that he can never escape. To be sure, for modern biographers of contemporary people, the job of checking details may appear to be relatively simple. All that is necessary is to get confirmation of the story from the people involved. Just ask the man who is reputed to have told the story in the first place. Unfortunately there always seem to be complications. Yet no competent scholar should accept any oral anecdotes without checking. The ways stories get changed with each retelling is fantastic. Let me give you a few examples to reinforce this point.

Recently, when collecting material for this book, I heard a dramatic story of misfortune. It came from a reputable source and sounded possible. Edgar Shannon, now President of the University of Virginia, so the tale went, while working years ago on Tennyson, heard of an ancient nanny, ninety years old, who had nursed the Tennyson children. When Shannon got in touch with her and asked whether she had any surviving relics of her years with the Tennysons, she replied: "I'm glad you came when you did, since last week I burned all my old letters. If you had come a few weeks ago I might have been tempted to show you all I had." Certainly a perfect example of a biographer's bad luck! Just the same, before I used it, I thought I had better check with Edgar Shannon himself, and dashed off a letter to him, apologizing for bothering a busy university president, but asking him to tell me if the account was correct. In a couple of weeks there came a reply, making a number of corrections. It had not been a nanny at all but an elderly nurse who had attended Tennyson in his last illness. But nothing was said about her remarks; so I wrote another letter to Shannon, specifically asking about what the nurse had said. Had she really been relieved that she did not have to make up her mind as to whether or not to show her papers? Back came another friendly reply, giving further details. The old nurse had had some half-dozen letters from Tennyson, but she had not thought them of any particular value. Now I quote Shannon's letter exactly: "in preparation for her family to be able to dispose of her remains easily at her death she had burned all her letters and other papers and personal memorabilia only a few weeks previous to my hearing about her." That was all. Nothing about any possible reluctance to show the letters to him, or any ethical qualms. And so all the delightful overtones go out of the anecdote, and only the bare bones remain. To be sure, the episode is still worth repeating as a sample of unfortunate timing. But the colorful trappings, with the unexpected suggestion at the end had obviously merely been added in casual repetitions of the story.

Another example has to do with the researches of a British military historian, Oliver Warner. When working on his life of Lord Nelson, he was curious as to the size of his subject's head (We biographers do sometimes have strange preoccupations!). According to the tale as I had it from a reputable English friend, Warner was walking down St. James's Street in London one day, when he passed an ancient firm making military uniforms. The thought suddenly struck him that it might be possible that some such firm would have made Nelson's uniforms, and might still have his measurements. And so, on an impulse, he walked into the shop, where he found an aged tailor sitting cross-legged on a table, hard at work. When Warner apologetically asked his question, the old tailor reached down and opened up a small trap door in the floor and called down to someone below: " 'Arry, send up Lord Nelson's account." In a few minutes, attached to a string on a pulley, up came a package of papers which contained all the admiral's measurements. You can imagine how pleased I was by this story, which so admirably illustrated the delights of what I have been calling "outside" research. But, just the same, I thought I had better check it if I could. A quick look at *Who's Who* showed me that Oliver Warner was living in Haslemere in Surrey. Off went another apologetic letter asking for more details about the episode. Very quickly there came back an answer, explaining exactly what had happened, and giving me three or four more anecdotes about his adventures following Nelson's trail. Here is the true story of what happened. Warner wrote:

> I wanted to find out whether Nelson's so-called "patch," which was really an eye-shade to protect his good eye from glare, could be investigated further. I called on Messrs Lock, of St. James's Street, to ask them if they had supplied Nelson's hats. Yes, they said, and we have his account, but it is on loan to Westminster Abbey, and there, in a little museum, was not only the splendid well known effigy of Nelson by Catherine Andras, but Lock's ledger, and one of the hats and shades involved, or a photograph of such, I forget which.

Vanished were the cross-legged tailor, the trap door and " 'Arry," the string and the pulley. Instead merely a trip to Westminster Abbey to see an exhibition there. Rather than an example of fortuitous accident, the story perfectly illustrates how anecdotes pick up embellishments in the telling.

Multiple versions of the same story are not so easy to check when everyone concerned has disappeared. Marchette Chute cites as an example the death of Sir Philip Sidney in the sixteenth century. It is known that he was killed in battle by a musket ball which shattered his thigh. Everyone agrees that he was vulnerable because that day he had not put on his leg armor. But why he had neglected to do so is not so clear. There are various explanations. Sir Fulke Greville says that because the Marshall of the Camp was not wearing leg armor Sidney, characteristically, refused to have any special advantage. A contemporary doctor, on the other hand, says that it was merely because Sidney had been in a hurry. And Sir John Smythe, a conservative military expert, blamed the tragedy on a misguided current craze for leaving off leg protection, a tendency he deeply deplored. Who was right? Marchette Chute solves the problem by examining the point of view of each of the authorities, trying to see what motives might have accounted for his point of view. Two of them, she suggests, were trying to prove a thesis—Greville wishing to illustrate Sidney's chivalric nature, and Smythe eager to prove the importance of leg armor in battle.

Only the doctor apparently had no axe to grind. Thus Miss Chute tends to think his explanation the closest to the truth.[4]

In this instance the biographer has been able to find some logical methods of differentiating between sources which disagree. Unfortunately this is not always possible. One of the most often quoted anecdotes concerning Samuel Johnson as a young man is about his quarrel with the bookseller Osborne, whom Johnson knocked down with a huge folio.[5] Most scholars, and I believe rightly, accept the basic story as correct. Johnson admitted as much to both Boswell and Mrs. Thrale. But where did the event occur? Mrs. Thrale implies that it happened in Osborne's shop, and most of the contemporary versions recounted by others agree. Yet Boswell quotes Johnson directly as saying that it was in his own chambers. This seems more likely, and with Boswell's known general reliability, most of us today accept this version. Many other examples could be adduced where the choice comes down to a question of the dependability of authorities.

There have been times when two diarists independently wrote down accounts of the same conversation. To compare the two versions can be fascinating. Consider this instance. As I pointed out earlier, on 5 April 1775, the Irish clergyman Thomas Campbell dined in the Poultry with the publishers Dilly, as a guest of Boswell, to meet Dr. Johnson. Both Campbell and Boswell kept fairly full accounts of the conversation that day. Dr. Campbell wrote: "Talking of Addisons timidity keeping him down so that he never spoke in the house of commons was he said much more blameworthy than if he had attempted & failed; as a man is more praise worthy who fights & is beaten than he who runs away." Boswell records the remark this way: "We talked of speaking in public. Mr. Johnson said that one of the first wits of this country, Isaac Hawkins Browne, got into Parliament and never opened his mouth. Mr. Johnson said that it was more disgraceful not to try to speak than to try and fail, as it was more disgraceful not to fight than to fight and be beat." The essentials are pretty much the same. Campbell says it was Addison, and Boswell says Isaac Hawkins Browne.

Might it not have been both? When discussing timidity, Johnson may well have cited both of the older wits, and each diarist selected the example which made more sense to him.[6]

The fact that Boswell was a Scot and Campbell an Irishman may in some instances account for the discrepancies in their recording of Johnson's remarks, and also what is stressed. For example, on 8 April the two diarists were together again at the Thrales in Southwark. At one point Campbell set down:

He seems fond of Boswell, & yet he is always abusing the Scots before him, by way of joke—talking of their nationality—he said they were not singular—The negros & Jews being so too.—Boswell lamented there was no good map of Scotland.—There never can be a good of Scotland, says the Doctor sententiously. This excited Boswell to ask wherefore. Why Sir to measure land a man must go over it; but who cd think of going over Scotland?

Boswell in his journal entry for that day makes no mention of this exchange, but on Good Friday, the 14th, he wrote:

When I put down Mr. Johnson's sayings, I do not keep strictly to chronology. I am glad to collect the gold dust, as I get by degrees as much as will be an ingot. I told him that Mr. Orme said many parts of the East Indies were better mapped than the Highlands of Scotland. Said Mr. Johnson: "That a country may be mapped, it must be travelled over." "Nay" said I, "can't you say it is not *worth* mapping?"

In the *Life of Johnson* Boswell later added an explanation of his last question: "Nay, (said I, meaning to laugh with him at one of his prejudices,) can't you say. . . ."[7]

On the 8th both diarists recorded another exchange concerning Barry the actor. Boswell's version is:

Mrs. Thrale told us that Mr. Johnson had said that Barry was just fit to stand at the door of an auction-room with a long pole: "Pray gentlemen, walk in." She said Murphy said Garrick was fit for that, and would pick your pocket after you came out. Mr. Johnson said there was no wit there "You may say of any man that he will pick a pocket. Besides, the man at the door does not pick pockets. That is to be done within by the auctioneer."

Campbell records it this way:

Mrs Thrale then took him by repeating a repartee of Murphy—(The setting Barry up in competition with Garric is what irritates the English Criticks) & Murphy standing up for Barry, Johnson said that he was fit for nothing but to stand at an auction room door with his pole &c— Murphy said that Garrick wd do the business as well & pick the people's pockets at the same time.—Johnson admitted the fact but said Murphy spoke nonsense for that peoples pockets were not picked at the door, but in the room &c &c—Then say'd I he was worse than the pick pocket, forasmuch as he was Pandar to them—this went off with a laugh—*vive la Bagatelle*.[8]

Essentially, again, the main points of the story are the same; only the embellishments are different. Campbell could not resist including his own supposedly humorous comment, quite understandably ignored by Boswell. Boswell, with his characteristic skill, gives Johnson's main remark, as told by their hostess, in dramatic form. Even when second or third hand, the remark becomes a part of the dramatic structure of the *Life*. Of course, it is easy to point out intriguing minor differences. But what is more important is the fact that in essentials both men give us the same story. When this occurs the biographer must heave a sigh of relief. If he tends to quote Boswell's version, with its additional color, he does have confirmation of the basic points from Campbell.

Unfortunately this is not always possible. An example of conflicting evidence may be found in an incident recounted by Mrs. Piozzi in her *Anecdotes of Dr. Johnson* in 1786. After giving some examples of Johnson's rough speeches, she recorded:

He was no gentler with myself, or those for whom I had the greatest regard. When I one day lamented the loss of a first cousin killed in America—"Prithee, my dear (said he), have done with canting: how would the world be worse for it, I may ask, if all your relations were at once spitted like larks, and roasted for Presto's supper?"[9]

Boswell, five years later, after commenting on Mrs. Piozzi's exaggeration and distortion and her tendency to paint Johnson as deficient in tenderness and ordinary civility, continued:

I allow that he made her an angry speech; but let the circumstances fairly appear, as told by Mr. Baretti, who was present:

'Mrs. Thrale, while supping very heartily upon larks, laid down her knife and fork, and abruptly exclaimed, "O, my dear Mr. Johnson, do you know what has happened? The last letters from abroad have brought us an account that our poor cousin's head was taken off by a cannon ball."

Johnson, who was shocked both at the fact, and her light unfeeling manner of mentioning it, replied, "Madam, it would give *you* very little concern if all your relations were spitted like those larks, and drest for Presto's supper.' "[10]

Millions of readers of the *Life*, impressed by Boswell's acknowledged accuracy, and by the lady's tarnished reputation, have assumed that she had distorted the story. But what of the real evidence? Boswell got his version from Baretti, not noted for veracity, and one who hated Mrs. Piozzi violently. He had shown his antipathy in a series of nasty articles, filled with fabrications. Can he be wholly believed? Years later, in the margins of two separate editions of the *Life of Johnson* Mrs. Piozzi scribbled her reactions to this passage.[11] In one she wrote: "Boswell appealing to Baretti for a Testimony of the *Truth* is comical enough"—"I never address'd him so familiarly *in my Life*. I never did eat any Supper:—& there were no Larks to eat"—"nor was ever a *hot dish* seen on the Table after Dinner at Streatham Park." In the other copy she repeated some of the same claims, adding: "& dar'd as well have swallow'd the Lark *alive* as have said O my dear Johnson! She never address'd him with any such familiarity."

It may well be that the true story lies somewhere between the two versions. Undoubtedly Mrs. Thrale's remark was made in a flippant manner, which irritated Johnson. She never denied this. But the background details provided by Baretti are probably all wrong. Boswell thus erred in accepting such a story from a known enemy of the lady. Although usually he checked carefully, this time his own desire to get back at Mrs. Piozzi led him to accept dubious evidence. Again, the modern scholar has to weigh the motives of each authority.

Elsewhere in the volumes she pointed out what she considered other errors of fact. In his entry for 28 April 1778 Boswell suggested that she was responsible for an alteration in Johnson's dress —a very reasonable guess, we might say. But she noted in the margin: "no truly—it was Mr. Thrale & not his Wife who attempted such Corrections. He would no more have suffer'd *me* to have chosen his Coat than the very Youngest of my Children."[12] And in April, 1781, when Boswell remarked that Johnson had removed "I suppose by the solicitation of Mrs. Thrale, to a house in Grosvenor-square," she added: "spiteful again; he went by Direction of his Physicians where they could easiest attend him."[13]

Again and again Boswell in the *Life* jibed at Mrs. Piozzi's inaccuracy, and in her annotations she kept defending herself. Appended to an account of the first occasion of Johnson's thinking in earnest of religion, Boswell referred in a footnote to "a strange fantastical account" given by Mrs. Piozzi. To this the lady exploded: "he told me this *himself*; I did not dream it, & could not have invented it, or heard it from others. I will *swear* he told me as I told the Public, & swear it (if they will) when in my last Moments. In 1808 *They* cannot be far distant."[14] Sometimes, of course, she confirmed what her rival was saying, as when Boswell records Johnson's own account of Tetty's admiration of *The Rambler*, and she adds in the margin: "He told me the same Thing in the same Words."[15]

Where Boswell admits that he is merely guessing, and Mrs. Thrale is the person cited, then her last word would appear to be more reliable. When it is merely a matter of two opposing opinions, then there is no easy way of determining the truth. Perhaps in each instance one should try to decide which witness had the best opportunity to observe what was going on.

Unfortunately, it is never a simple matter to evaluate the authenticity of each authority and then use the account which seems the more reliable. Often there is no way of determining where the story started. As it is passed along, each anecdote changes subtly, and it is quite possible that the careless change of a single word may distort the whole meaning.

Yet it is the duty of the biographer to attempt some kind of analysis. First there is the matter of external corroboration, with proof that specific facts were wrong, or that there are other stories of a similar nature which may have been the source. Should the originator of the anecdote be known, there may be a way to discover some pattern of accuracy in his accounts. At least we can tell what was his relationship to the subject of the life, whether he had any obvious reason to falsify this particular story, or whether the tale is told carelessly or in full dress. If the original author is unknown, one may guess from the style what kind of a person he was—serious minded or frivolous. And we can try to find any signs of bias or evidence of how well he knew the subject. When did his version first appear?

The number of versions on one side need not be conclusive. They may all have ultimately come from a single unreliable source. Wallace Notestein proposes as an example the estimate of a man of whom six records say approximately the same thing, and one diary gives an utterly different judgment.[16] Although it would be hard to reject what might appear to be an almost unanimous opinion, yet Notestein insists the biographer must be prepared to do just that. The decision has to be tested by every sort of external evidence. If in the end the one version does seem to have the most validity, it should be accepted and the others discarded.

In Dr. Johnson's life of Swift, which appeared in 1781, he tells of Swift's early attempts to write Pindaric odes in the Cowleyan manner, and of his showing some of them to Dryden, who was a distant relative. Johnson concluded: "I have been told that Dryden, having perused these verses, said, 'Cousin Swift, you will never be a poet'; and that this denunciation was the motive of Swift's perpetual malevolence to Dryden."[17] Dryden's pointed remark, phrased in Johnson's own emphatic style, has been repeated countless times.

But Maurice Johnson has shown that we cannot be sure of exactly what Dryden said. The first appearance of the story in print came in 1753 in the *Lives of the Poets of Great Britain*, officially assigned to Theophilus Cibber, but usually attributed to Robert Shiels. Here the remark is given as: "Cousin Swift, turn your thoughts some other way, for nature has never formed you for a Pindarick poet."[18] The two renderings have one very essential difference—the omission by Johnson of the single word "Pindarick"—which changes the whole import of the story. As we are quite willing to accept, Swift was not suited to be a lyric poet, but he did later become a great verse satirist. He was a major poet, but of a particular kind. Thus if Dryden said something like "Cousin Swift, you will never be a Pindarick Poet," then he spoke the truth and we would all agree. But if the descriptive adjective is omitted, we who have later knowledge would say that Dryden was wrong, and Swift, in later years, did have cause to hold a grudge.

The question still remains as to which is the more reliable version. No one can tell exactly where Shiels got his account in the first place. It may even have been from Johnson, who passed on the story which he had heard somewhere, Shiels setting it down in his own rather flat style. Years later Johnson remembered the incident, and told it in his own incisive, forceful manner, omitting the adjective since he felt he had made clear in the earlier part of the passage that it was the lyric odes which had been submitted to Dryden.

As a general rule, the biographer, like the textual editor who depends for wording and accidentals on the first edition of a work, should try to discover the earliest version of each anecdote. Even if apparently impossible, the attempt must be made. In the instance just recounted, Shiels's version could hardly have come directly from someone who had overheard the remark of Dryden's. He must have been merely quoting third or fourth hand, and thus his version cannot claim any unimpeachable authority. Nor can Johnson's. When such is the case, I suggest that it is the duty of the biographer to describe the scene as best he can, citing the basic differences between the two versions, and then suggesting that Dryden probably did mean his remark to apply only to the Pindaric odes which he had been shown. If this seems weaseling and wordy, I cannot help it. The biographer's duty is to reproduce the truth as closely as he humanly can.[19]

One way out of such a difficulty, of course, is to print all the various accounts and let the reader decide. Some modern life-writers follow this procedure, but it wastes a great deal of space, and is basically an evasion of responsibility. Or the biographer can argue the matter at length in a long footnote. Or he can try to evolve some sort of fusion between the accounts and re-create what he thinks must have happened. Actually, conflation of this sort is always risky.[20] Perhaps here the whole decision depends upon what kind of biography is being produced—one which aims to be selective and interpretative, or one which is intended to give all the facts.

7. Form—Types of Biography

৯৯ Before he does anything else a biographer has to decide what kind of a book he is going to write, and foresee its potential audience. He cannot select his evidence or choose a style, or make any of his difficult choices, until he knows just what form his work will take. Yet this is not as simple as it may seem. Today we tend to emphasize that rather than a single definable kind of life-writing, there are widely different kinds. But how to differentiate among the multiplicity of possible approaches has never been determined.

Often it has been implied that the distinction is merely between popular and scholarly lives, the basis for judgment being the presence or absence of footnotes and bibliographies and whether the approach is sober and methodical, or chatty and informal. Yet such a simple distinction ignores many other factors. Some critics have suggested that it is all a matter of the use of sources. For subjects who lived long ago, like Chaucer and Shakespeare, where the amount of evidence concerning personal affairs may be minimal, all that can be done is to produce what Marchette Chute calls "silhouette" biography. Here the subject is a two-dimensional figure shown in a colorful and carefully drawn setting. Emphasis is on background, not character. Or for modern subjects, where evidence is plentiful, there is the question of how much to use, whether every scrap of information, from manuscripts as well as early editions is sought, or whether dependence is solely on secondary sources.

A third possible basis for categorization might be the amount of interpretation done by the author, whether he conscientiously attempts to be objective, merely presenting the facts, or, on the other hand, tries to get inside his subject's mind and seek the reasons behind his actions. And if he interprets, whether he should be an Olympian story-teller who knows all, or a critical intelligence making judgments, analyses, and interpretations.[1]

Admittedly, there are many other possible methods of evaluation, each with merit but inconclusive when taken by itself. I will not attempt to enumerate them. Instead, I should like to suggest a series of five categories for biography, beginning with the so-called "objective" and ending with the "subjective." The trouble is that the kind of terminology generally used to explain literary and political differences, as they move on a scale from one extreme to another, will not work for my five divisions. Hard to soft, high to low, right to left—none of these is suitable. There would be howls of protest if I labeled fictional biography as "far left" or "far right" or "high" or "low." And to name five gradations of subjectivity is just as hard. Thus I shall attempt to describe each of the types, without any uniformity in the labels.

To begin with so-called "objective" biography there is the controversial question of whether it is possible at all. There must always be, we might say, some personal choice made by the author. He has to decide what to put in, since a purely mechanical assemblage of all the relevant evidence is in practice an impossibility. Yet it must be admitted that there have been a few attempts to do just this, to assemble everything relating to some person and present it without editorial comment or structure. Edward Nehls's *D. H. Lawrence: A Composite Biography* (1957–59) is an example. J. Milton French's *Life Records of John Milton* (1949–58) and Jay Leyda's *Melville Log* (1951) are others. Leyda's exhaustive researches provided the ground work for Leon Howard's *Herman Melville* (1951). Nehls claims to be making no subjective choices, serving merely as a researcher who gathers together in one place all the available evidence, and passes it on to the reader without further comment. But even he has been selective. Although he prints everything he can find which bears directly on his subject, there must also be other important details—inferences, casual remarks of other people, oblique approaches—none of which focuses on Lawrence, but which might be relevant to his personality. Many of these Nehls has left out. Only if one could do the impossible—collect everything which in any way touched on the life of the subject, or his friends, involving all the ideas of the period, the history of the epoch—could there be complete lack of personal involvement on the part of the author. The best that can be said, then, for this first category is that it represents only partial, or selective objectivity.

Next on the scale I would place what we usually think of as "scholarly-historical" biography. There is always some selection of evidence, but no unacknowledged guesswork, no fictional devices, and no attempts to interpret the subject's personality and actions psychologically. The basic technique is careful use of selected facts, strung together in chronological order, with some historical background. As samples, I might list Dumas Malone's *Jefferson*, Douglas Freeman's *Washington*, or Leslie Marchand's *Byron*. Of course there are differing gradations, depending somewhat on the character of the subject. Ernest Jones's *Freud* must differ somewhat in technique from Gordon Ray's *Thackeray*, and Newman White's *Shelley* from Arthur S. Link's *Woodrow Wilson*. The chief point is that few risks are taken. Although scholarly biographers do obviously make some subjective choices, they always try to be fair, and hope that the reader will himself understand what is going on. When guesswork is necessary it is openly confessed.

The third division might be called "artistic-scholarly" biography. It involves the same exhaustive research, but once the evidence has been assembled, the biographer considers his role that of an imaginative creative artist, presenting the details in the liveliest and most interesting manner possible. There is no conscious distortion of evidence, or making up of conversations or events. It is merely that the life-writer thinks of himself as more than a historian. As Leon Edel puts it, "The biographer may be as imaginative as he pleases—the more imaginative the better—in the way in which he brings his materials together. But he must not imagine the materials. He must read himself into the past; but then he must read that past into our present."[2]

My *Young Sam Johnson* was intended to fit this description. My life of Mrs. Piozzi, on the other hand, is clearly in the second division. For *Young Sam* I tried to follow the procedures outlined just above. Year after year I kept searching for every available bit of evidence, but once I began to write, my mind was fastened on my audience. How could I use the evidence in the most imaginative way, and tell the story as smoothly as possible? Obviously this meant taking some risks. And it meant doing some structuring of evidence. As an example, let me cite the opening of the first chapter, where I describe the fifty-five-year-old Johnson sitting down to begin writing an account of his early years. In the text I do not give my authorities, but I had what I considered dependable evidence for everything I said. In the year 1765 Boswell set down a very detailed description of just how Johnson's head shook and his body moved back and forth, how he made various noises or talked to himself, and how he rubbed his knee with the palm of his hand—all this whenever he wrote. And, as far as we know, it was in this same year that he began to write the little autobiographical fragment describing his own life up to his eleventh year. Thus it seemed justifiable to combine the two for a graphic opening. But there was a distinct risk since the absolute dating of the autobiographical fragment is uncertain. Unfortunately the manuscript has disappeared, and all we know about it comes from the rare first printing by Richard Wright in 1805. In a note in this provincial printing, the editor says "This was written in January, 1765," but whether the reference is to a late addition at that point or to the original account is uncertain. I chose the literal interpretation which suited me best, and I still think that I was right. But suppose this manuscript finally turns up, and it becomes clear that Johnson had actually begun his account way back in the forties, and not in '65, as I assume. My use of Boswell's colorful description would not be justified, for his eccentricities might not have been so far developed twenty years earlier. The whole opening of my book might thus be rendered dubious. Even though this would be extremely embarrassing, I decided to take the risk because I believed I was right and it offered me a dramatic opening for my book. Elsewhere, too, I took similar risks in establishing chronology. Naturally, in the notes I indicate my sources so that the reader can check them if he wishes. But in the text I thought it defensible to tell the story as well as I could, though never consciously fabricating dialogue or imagining scenes which might never have happened.

The fourth division I call "narrative" biography. This is the type made popular by Catherine Drinker Bowen in her early books (in her latest she has become more conservative). Very popular have been her delightful accounts of Tchaikowsky, *Beloved Friend*, Justice Oliver Wendell Holmes, *Yankee from Olympus*, and *John Adams*. She starts with immense enthusiasm, and engages in extensive research. In various places she has described some of her adventures in trailing manuscripts and controversial evidence.[3] But once she has collected all the evidence, she turns it into a running narrative, almost fictional in form. There are dramatic scenes and conversations, which create the atmosphere of real life. Not that she makes up the conversations, for she always has documentary support for what she does. She merely turns passages in letters or diaries into dialogue. Suppose in a letter A tells about an amusing talk he had with B and C. Instead of quoting this letter, Mrs. Bowen is more likely to take the account and bring it into her book as an actual conversation among the three. To be sure, the subject matter is the same, but the effect has been made more vivid. The biographer in the fourth division, then, does allow some subjective imagination on his part to add color to his narration, though he does not indulge in pure fiction.

In the fifth division, on the other hand, imagination is given full rein. The fictional biographer thinks of himself almost as novelist. He sees no need to do extensive research, since the scholars have done that for him. Thus he tends to rely on secondary sources, and believes it in his province to turn the dry historical sources into literature. When there are blanks in our knowledge he makes up what is necessary. He supplies long conversations and imagines background. The result reads like a novel, and largely is one. Although a real person who actually lived is the hero, most of the details and the important scenes come right out of the mind of the novelist-biographer. The very popular books of Irving Stone might serve as examples—*Lust for Life* (Van Gogh), *The Agony and the Ecstasy* (Michelangelo), and *Love is Eternal* (Mary Todd Lincoln). These life stories are largely subjective creations of Stone, using miscellaneous information which he has collected through casual reading, but they could hardly be called authentic reference works.

I could mention other books in this same category. Perhaps a passage from one—a life of Dryden by Kenneth Young, which appeared in 1954—may characterize the type. Chapter XI begins this way:

The first leaves of Autumn are falling in the garden of Lord Leicester's great mansion as the front door of a new house on its northern side opens, and two old gentlemen carefully descend the steps into the street. Behind them, an old woman with streaky grey hair, close-set eyes, and a discontented expression closes the door with a bang; the shorter, more portly, of the two men, who is carrying a sheaf of papers, sighs.

The two slowly turn the corner into Little Newport Street, and make towards the Strand; then the taller, who has an air of authority and an assertive way of pushing his chin forward, remarks: "You are to have Mrs. Bracegirdle and Mrs. Mountfort this time—not a patch on Nelly Gwin nor on Annie Reeves. Pah, they can't act no more!"

"Dear Robert," says his plump, rubicund companion, "they never *could* act, those women...."

One scarcely need point out that the whole of this scene comes from the biographer's imagination.

In a recent life of Milton by Edmund Fuller the same general technique is used. Fuller's method is thus summed up by a *Times Literary Supplement* reviewer:

Quotation is necessary to convey the quality of this book. We learn early that any sunny afternoon in 1626 "was likely to find Milton dickering with the avaricious watermen who rowed spectators to the theatres and bearpits along the Thames." At Cambridge his pen drips with "bitter and satiric writings which curled the hair of his teachers." Life at Horton is more tranquil and dawn often finds Milton "watching the flaming sunrise and chatting with the plowman or shepherd. . . . Mower and milkmaid saw him wandering as they worked." His father is worried by his dilatoriness, but shows the appropriate tolerance: " 'your sonnet is good, John. . . . I will not interfere.' "[4]

Fuller admits that in order to interpret his subject's complex nature his book "employs some of the techniques of the novel," but insists that in every case his fictional scenes "have been based upon the established facts of Milton's life, or derived from opinions expressed in his writings." Certainly this kind of writing represents the opposite pole from Nehls's mere assembling all the evidence about D. H. Lawrence. Yet each kind claims, in one way or another, to be biography.

On such a scale as I suggest, it is hard to know just where to place the ironical, sometimes vindictive, character studies of Lytton Strachey, the essays of Gamaliel Bradford, or the *New Yorker* profiles. They are neither fiction nor objective biography. Perhaps I should have provided a sixth category especially designed for such works. Or they could be put in a special subdivision of the third type, "artistic-scholarly" biography. Admittedly, they do not at all represent the kind of detailed research which I envisage as necessary for the best productions of this kind, but they are creative and based on genuine evidence. They are a special type and should be so considered.

Another work difficult to place is Virginia Woolf's *Orlando*. Although it pretends to be a biography, and we know had a real person as its subject, it is more fictional than most of those listed in my fifth category. With its mockery of time and history, its pretense to scholarship and lighthearted take-offs, it is, Leon Edel suggests, basically a "literary lark," a "fantasy in the form of biography."[5]

ಶಿ

Having suggested this five-part differentiation of types, I propose now to concentrate largely on Type III, which is the one most appealing to the creative biographer. As I have indicated, he must have complete mastery of historical details; he cannot be casual in research or slovenly in workmanship. But he is permitted qualified manipulation of facts for the dramatic re-creation of his subject's career. Some risks may be taken, provided the reader is aware of what is going on. On the other hand, nothing can be invented, or completely imagined.

Of the basic problems which face a biographer planning a work of this kind, first and foremost is the matter of chronology. In what order should the material be presented? To put it another way, how many liberties may an author take with strict historical sequence? Does he have to begin with his subject's ancestry and birth, and then carry him, chapter by chapter, through to his death, giving all the facts just as they occurred? Or are there other ways to tell the story?

In literature there has never been any agreement as to how to tell a story. The ancient epic began *in medias res*, and through various devices necessary details concerning earlier events are brought in later. For ordinary fiction, from classical times on down, chronological order was in more general use—at least in romances, lives of criminals, and edifying tales. Defoe takes his heroes and heroines in a straight line from early life to death, and the great novelists of the mid-eighteenth century in general follow suit. Even though *Pamela* may appear to begin in the middle the major part of the book is told in chronological order. It was not until Laurence Sterne that natural sequence is discarded, and psychological order is substituted. It is what goes on in the mind of the fictional character Tristram Shandy that counts—what suddenly pops out of his subconscious, or is suggested by some other idea. The book jumbles together in fantastic disarray events which occurred long before the hero's birth with accounts of his conception and his later career. On a single page there may be allusions to unrelated events forty years apart. Even more in the modern stream-of-consciousness fiction of Virginia Woolf and James Joyce is the old-fashioned orderly sequence of events replaced by something more psychologically realistic. But can this type of presentation also be used in biography? That is another matter, and it has never been satisfactorily examined.

In many ways the serious biographer and the novelist have much in common. Both claim to present life in the truest sense. One uses imagined events, the other discovered ones. Both are faced with similar problems—how to create a semblance to life out of facts, ideas, and words—how to give the illusion of living, with all its variety and richness. Novelists, it may be pointed out, have discovered ways of suggesting depth and ambiguity through various narrative devices and the use of symbols and patterns of behavior, sometimes even through myths and archetypes. Is it possible that the life writer could also use these techniques? We know that every man who has ever lived works from his own set of symbols and his responses to them, that he has his own subconscious motivations and drives. The question is whether a biographer of someone who lived years ago can possibly discover these fundamental forces in his subject. And if he can, how can he make them clear to a modern reader?

Obviously it is impossible for us to get inside the mind of a dead person, or to follow exactly the wandering thoughts of one who is living. But it may be legitimate, by using flashbacks or résumés, to pull together material from different periods in a subject's life. Nothing need be made up, nothing fabricated, but through the use of a well-known fictional technique an effect may be achieved which is similar to that of a novelist. The reader could be brought closer to the subject, and given an inkling of the way his mind might have worked, if the subject had attempted his own autobiography. Frankly, I know no biographer who has worked completely along these lines. It might be interesting to see one try.

There are those, however, who violate strict chronology in other ways and are able to produce something of the same effect. Leon Edel's life of Henry James, in five successive installments, is a good example. The first volume appeared in 1953; the second and third in 1962; the fourth in 1969.[6] The fifth and final volume is now almost done. Five volumes devoted to a man who had a singularly uneventful life! How does Edel hold the reader's interest—as he surely does? Not by any matter-of-fact piling up of facts, or any routine plodding narrative! Of course, Edel has an enormous amount of material from which to select. James was an accomplished letter writer, and he had many famous friends. Edel's art is in structuring his evidence, seizing on crucial themes and building them up irrespective of simple chronology. Naturally he begins with James's family and youth. Each volume moves through consecutive periods. But within these periods he takes great liberties with time, arranging his material in the light of psychological patterns forming and reforming. The reader does feel that he is actually accompanying a real person through his life; not merely following his day-to-day actions, but getting inside his mind and evaluating his motives.

On one occasion Edel talked to me at length about his theory of life-writing, and he gave me the reasons behind some of his violations of strict chronology. The last sections of his Volume III stressed two very important episodes in James's life—the suicide in Venice of his friend Miss Constance Fenimore Woolson, and his own involvement in the dispersal of her manuscripts; and preparations for the production of the play *Guy Domville*. Thus Volume III ends: "At Christmas of 1894, when one of the most tragic years of his life approached its end, he waited for the rising of the curtain on his new play—and on his future."

In concentrating on what he considered the most significant of the forces affecting James during this period, Edel chose to ignore a number of other matters, though they too were important, and let them wait until he was ready for them. These were the death of Stevenson, his increasing friendship with the actress Elizabeth Robins, the arrival of Kipling, and other events. Volume IV picks up all these loose threads. Instead of moving directly to the performance of *Guy Domville*, as the reader may well have expected, Edel moves back in a series of flashbacks to the beginning of James's dramatic involvement, to his increasing interest in Ibsen and his friendship for the actress. In a series of chapters, often going back a number of years, he returns to all of these old themes. All this in retrospect! It is not until over fifty pages of this kind of filling in that we finally come to the exciting first night of the play.

Of course, all this adds to the suspense, but Edel's reasoning is that while he was telling the tragic story of Miss Woolson and its effect on James he could not stop to discuss other matters. He wanted Volume III to end on this traumatic event. But before he could go on to James's failure as a dramatist it was necessary to fill in the background which had temporarily been ignored. Thus the delay served two purposes.

Similarly, Volume V picks up other material omitted in Volume IV. James first met H. G. Wells in 1898 and began to see a good deal of him in 1899. But it was not until 1912 that their relationship began to move into a critical stage. Then it was that Wells began to argue against James's fictional method. In 1914, in an article in *TLS*, James took Wells apart, and Wells replied by satirizing James in *Boon*. Although Edel casually mentions the first meetings of the two men, he postpones until Volume V the description of their long friendship and its breaking up, going back over fifteen years to pull everything together. In this way he can tell the whole story dramatically, rather than bit by bit in strict chronology. Such an approach allows the casual reader the satisfaction of seeing in advance the fundamental reasons behind the final explosion.

Another example: James met Joseph Conrad as early as 1897, but Volume IV ends in 1901 with only incidental mentions of Conrad. What Volume IV does is to move James out into the country, stressing his loneliness and disappointments. Edel does not clutter it up with any discussion of his life at Rye. But Volume V begins with all these details. Here there is a great deal about his past friendships with other novelists living in the neighborhood—with Ford Madox Ford, Stephen Crane, Conrad, and others. Ford and Conrad are totally dealt with here, each with a chapter in chronological order as James had met them. But H. G. Wells, though introduced into the chapter on Crane, is given fuller treatment near the end of the volume when the whole argument of Wells and James is summed up in detail.

The plan of Volume V very much resembles that of IV—a series of chapters using the retrospective method, before moving into the progressive narrative of James's life. Actually, the flashback technique can appear at any time in Edel's scheme of things. He is very adept, too, in the way he foreshadows later events. With a hint here, a veiled suggestion there, the reader is prepared for what follows.

Edel is very careful not to quote long segments of letters, since they usually deal with too many subjects. Many biographers insist on quoting complete letters in their chronological place, with the result that the reader's attention is scattered among many themes, incidents, and events. For instance, Ellmann, in his life of Joyce, includes many long quotations, and the reader may find it difficult to carry in his mind all the details. Thematic continuity is consequently rendered more difficult. Edel, instead, puts in only those portions which are relevant for the particular theme he is at that moment stressing. Other matters may be used later in their proper place.

Edel simply refuses to be bound by any arbitrary framework of events. He may even, when he first began writing, have had no definite idea of just how long his biography would be, or just what would be included. His purpose was to give the reader as complete and revealing a picture of James as possible, and with this in mind to arrange the telling in as dramatic a form as possible. To be sure, in such restructuring of time, as Edel himself admits, he has to be very careful about the tenses of his verbs.

It must be obvious to everyone that Edel's technique cannot be used on any kind of a subject; it only works where there is a great mass of material available, and with certain kinds of people. But with the right sort, it does have fascinating possibilities. By using flashback techniques, and filling in material originally left out, the biographer could, in theory, go on almost forever. Indeed, it is tempting to compare this approach to that of Laurence Sterne in *Tristram Shandy*. You will remember that Sterne threw overboard chronological order altogether. Even though the ending had probably been envisaged almost from the very beginning, Sterne was able to fill in the middle ad infinitum. There was always something to remember, something to dredge up out of someone's past, whether Uncle Toby's or Tristram's or Le Fever's. When Sterne finally became tired he stopped and gave us the predestined ending. Of course, Leon Edel's biography of James could hardly be called Sternean, for he does follow a leisurely progress through separate periods, and does not throw away all sense of chronology. But the point I am making is that with our twentieth-century concentration on psychology and on character analysis, unrestricted by normal sequence of events, the possibilities of rounding out character portrayal, even in life-writing, become endless.

I have used Leon Edel as my example, but it would be easy to point out other modern biographers who have been experimenting with similar flashback techniques and other narrative devices taken over from the novelists. On the other hand, there are some very successful modern biographers who keep rigidly to chronology. Take Richard Ellmann's life of James Joyce, for example. His Table of Contents is merely a long list of dates—1904–1905, 1905, 1905–1906, 1906–1907, and so on. There are only three apparent digressions, where Ellmann delves into the backgrounds for *Ulysses* and other works. For the rest he follows the Joyce family along month by month, and whenever possible, day by day. At times he sketches in past events, fills in necessary gaps, but the relentless structure is the calendar. Although fundamentally un-Joycean, this seemed to Ellmann to be the best technique for his biography, and it undoubtedly is for others.

Another problem appears in the lives of productive literary figures. Here the main consideration is the matter of how to handle the subject's published works, whether they should be made subsidiary throughout, or should dominate the stage. It is not an easy decision, and there is much difference of opinion among practicing biographers. Of course, a life-writer may rigidly exclude all critical examination of a writer's works, and concentrate solely on the events of his life and family relationships. As he moves along, the author can mention the appearance of each work, stressing how much money it brought, and how many good or bad reviews, and then dash on to what happened next. This is certainly one way to handle the problem, but I hardly think it the best.

Most serious biographers will take another tack, believing that when the subject is an author to leave out critical analysis of his books is seriously to distort his life. Where the major portion of a man's existence is spent in creating works of art, it is necessary for the reader to be given some insight into his creative imagination, and some evaluation of his ability. But the nagging question still remains as to how the works should be handled. Ought the biographer to stop the account every so often in order to interpose critical studies of the works? Or should he attempt to weave his evaluation subtly into the narrative? The first I call the "stop and go" method, the second, the "interwoven." In this second technique the author tries to lure the reader into some aesthetic involvement with the writer and his work while still telling the story of his subject's career, through a short excerpt here, an allusion there, or a series of short analyses. With the first approach the reader is clearly told by the chapter headings when he is to expect a critical evaluation of a piece of literature. Thus the reader is given a free choice: if he is excited about what is going to happen next, he can skip over the critical sections and return to them later. One writer who follows the "stop and go" technique amusingly told me that his daughter, in college at the time, quickly read through the critical chapters and then later returned to the biographical parts. For most readers, however, I suspect common practice would be the other way around.

As an example of the "stop and go" method, take Irvin Ehrenpreis's life of Swift. In the first volume, which records Swift's early life, when we come to any major literary work such as the *Tale of a Tub* volume, the narrative stops and we are given five critical chapters—three on the *Tale*, one on the *Battle of the Books*, and one on the *Mechanical Operation of the Spirit*—some sixty pages. After that is over, the reader is brought back to Swift's career, and we move forward chronologically. Of course, in these sections some biographical material is introduced, but the main emphasis is on the works.

Michael Holroyd's *Lytton Strachey* might be cited as another example of the "stop and go" technique. Recently he admitted that at the start he wanted to do an analysis of Strachey's works, but as he began to write he became fascinated with his life. So he changed his approach and did a biographical study, with critical evaluations included as digressive chapters.[7]

Another, perhaps better known instance, is Edgar Johnson's *Charles Dickens* (1952), where there are alternating narrative and critical chapters. In his *Sir Walter Scott* (1970) there is a similar structure, although Johnson admits that this time he used a different method of composition. With Dickens he did it all in sequence— that is, when he came to *David Copperfield* he stopped and wrote the literary evaluation of the work, and then went on with the story of Dickens's life. When the next novel came along, the same procedure was followed. But with Scott he left all ten critical sections to be written last, after the main narrative was all done. When I chanced to talk to him he had completed seven, and had only three to go. The biographical part was already in the hands of the publishers, the critical parts to be inserted later in their proper places.

When I asked him why he had changed his procedure this way, he explained that the shifting back and forth between narrative and critical chapters slowed down his writing. He had found it more convenient to do the latter last. I might have asked him why the same kind of objection might not be offered on behalf of the reader. Does not the constant alternation between styles and techniques also slow down the reader? Edgar Johnson would surely have refused to admit such a possibility, for his main defense of the method is based on the claim that he does integrate the critical chapters into the narrative. These chapters are not simply analyses of the novels as works of literature which could be taken out and published separately. Each is intimately tied into the personality and character of the author. Thus there should be no problem of adjustment.

As an analogy, Johnson suggested (in a later letter) that the relationship between the biographer and the reader is something like that between the leader in a dance and his partner. To anything that the good leader initiates the good partner responds, with little conscious effort. For the moment he is a willing follower, hardly aware that he is being led into a different step.

To be sure, Johnson does claim to be using a very special kind of biographical criticism. For example, when he came to *David Copperfield* in the life of Dickens, he examined it as an evocation of Dickens's own personality. There is a constant projection to be seen of Dickens in his own works. So many of the characters in his novels are orphans, and in this fact Johnson sees his unconscious rejection of his own parents. There is, then, a back-and-forth relationship between Dickens and his characters.

Pip in *Great Expectations* is an example of the same kind of projection, and there is, throughout the novels, a constant probing of the parent-child relationship. It is useful to see how this develops throughout Dickens's life, and only through careful analysis of the novels can this be done. Thus the back-and-forth method is very important both for the biographer and the reader. The same, Johnson insists, holds true for Scott. In a way, then, Johnson claims his to be a special case.

Would the same hold true for Swift? Is Ehrenpreis's use of the "stop-and-go" technique to be justified on the same grounds? Is a complete analysis of the structure and content of *A Tale of a Tub* as necessary for our understanding of the character of Swift as is that of *David Copperfield* for Dickens? There is no easy answer. But at least this is an area which needs much more detailed discussion.

8. The Biographer's Involvement ஜௌ

Having decided what kind of biography to attempt—a decision which obviously affects all later choices—the biographer must then face the problem of just what material to use: how much to quote, what kinds of excerpts to use, what topics to stress, how seriously to attempt over-all characterization. He must make up his mind as to which passages in his subject's works are the most significant. But how does the author decide what is significant? What inner voice tells him to quote this sentence and not that? By what authority does he ignore one series of letters and concentrate on another?

The problem is first of all centered on the motivation of the biographer, not on the evidence itself. If his aim is simply to provide chronology for a running narrative, then the procedure need not be too complex, being chiefly that of establishing exact dates and checking the reliability of authorities. On the other hand, when any attempt is made to assess the character of one's subject, or to guess at his inner motives, then the process becomes more involved. At this point there is a subtle interaction between the life-writer himself and his material. The character of the biographer thus becomes of central importance—his inner motives, his own prejudices, his purpose in writing the life. And it is this very intricate double relationship of the biographer to his subject which needs to be studied. Some critics have, to be sure, pointed out the importance of the problem, but we need more critical analyses of just how this relationship of author and subject works in biography. No practicing biographer that I know of has ever tried to examine thoroughly the pressures which were behind all of his decisions.

As I have shown earlier, many historians in the past have too blandly assumed that they could be completely objective. Today we are much more skeptical. One reviewer even goes so far as to insist that "the past has no existence other than that which our minds can give it. That is why the historian, whether he intends to or not, molds the past in the image of his own personality—Gibbon, Michelet, Churchill—and that is why the historian differs only in degree, only in the openness of his intervention, from the historical novelist."[1] Others obviously would not go so far, though the importance of the subjective factor, whether conscious or unconscious, in the re-creation of the past is now generally accepted.

A few years ago the thought struck me that it might be worthwhile to interview a number of successful modern biographers to find out how aware they were of what they were doing. By this I mean whether they were conscious as they wrote of the various pressures which were exerted upon or within themselves, and of the basic reasons for each choice they were making. I was curious as to whether practicing life-writers thought as much about form and the creative experience as did novelists and poets. Since I was spending a sabbatical year in England, the time seemed propitious for such an investigation. I had no intention of having formal interviews with these biographers. I did not take along a tape recorder or secretary to record exactly what was said, but over a cup of tea or lunch at the Athenaeum I hoped to draw out some confessions. Then I planned, like Boswell, to run home and write down the substance of what had been said.

It proved to be a fascinating year, though I did not see as many writers as I had hoped. Dr. Johnson kept usurping too much time. Still, my notes of the interviews which I was able to arrange make stimulating reading. I am still not quite sure what I proved, for there was no discernible consensus, no general agreement as to aims and methods. Nevertheless I think it might be worthwhile to describe some of the talks and try to sum up what was said.

First I should give some idea of the nature of the questions I sprung on my unsuspecting luncheon companions. Some of the queries tried to probe their basic convictions as to actual methods—such matters as whether they carefully planned the form and structure of their work before they began to write, whether, as they moved along, they were aware of the reasons behind their important decisions, or whether they realized at any time that subjective judgment was involved. There were other questions, as to whether they were conscious of having set up at the start some over-all characterization of their subject, and had then tried to fit the evidence into this framework. I was curious, too, to know how much their view of their subject had changed as they wrote the books. There was also the nagging question as to how aware they had been, as they collected all their evidence, of recurring themes which illumined their subject's life.

Such questions probed the biographer's own self-awareness as he wrote. But there were other approaches. I kept asking whether they consciously searched for symbols or Jungian archetypal patterns of behavior, and if they did, how valid they thought they were. And I asked if they were convinced that there were other devices which the biographer could use which would give his work the same depth of meaning as can be found in a novel. Is it possible, I would ask, for the life-writer to play with levels of meaning and still be true to his subject?

In addition there were other kinds of questions which had to do with varying standards for different types of biography. I was naturally curious to know if these professional men would agree with me in thinking it wrong to claim biography as a single definable genre. The most difficult question of all, and one which I found it hard to make completely clear to my luncheon guests, had to do with how much the ordinary general reader needs to know about the subtle choices facing the life-writer. In the future will critical readers of serious biography concern themselves with the same kind of intricate explication of symbols and layers of meaning, as readers of fiction?

As might have been expected, the replies varied from startled surprise to baffled irritation. Not one of the distinguished biographers with whom I talked that year would admit to having thought deeply about the topics I was bringing up. None of them had any very convincing answers for me to write down. There certainly was no discernable agreement on anything. The only conclusion which I carried away from my series of talks was that the best biographers considered themselves creative artists. They recognized no general rules and thought very little about critical theories. As one friend later remarked to me, apparently life-writing is the last major discipline uncorrupted by criticism.

Each writer would confess to having read at one time or other some book on biography or some articles, though he would not agree that this had influenced him materially. Imagine a modern novelist who had not absorbed some criticism of the work of Joyce or Proust or Faulkner. Or a poet who had not argued over the techniques of T. S. Eliot, or Yeats, or Hopkins. Yet I found these biographers singularly unaware of the subtle problems of structure and techniques. Thus in one way my series of interviews was more disillusioning than enlightening.

It should be added that later on I did have very illuminating talks with some practicing biographers who had thought deeply about these problems, but these men had themselves written a good deal about the art of biography and usually were teachers with academic connections. Writers like Leon Edel and Edgar Johnson have developed coherent theories about life-writing, and have tried in their own works to embody the organizing principles they have evolved. For the most part, however, the British writers I first approached would not admit such disciplined behavior.

First I had a number of talks with serious-minded historians, who thought themselves completely objective and impartial. They insisted that they collected all the available evidence, weighed its validity, and then presented for the reader what was relevant in a straightforward chronological account. When I kept asking them why they had chosen this piece of evidence and not that, they became a bit annoyed, and kept reiterating that the reasons for choice almost always had to do with the intrinsic color and interest of the material. Here was a revealing anecdote, which obviously had to be included since it showed so much about the subject's character. And here was one which might easily be left out since it added nothing new. It was usually as simple as that. They were reluctant to admit that the choice was connected with any preconceived notion of what the subject's character had been, or that they applied evaluative standards. Yet when finally pinned to the wall, they had to confess that the choices were personal ones, and must have represented an attempt to put together some coherent character portrayal which had gradually evolved in their minds. Nevertheless, they kept insisting that their purpose was to present a sober, historical account, and they were horrified at the suggestion that they might have warped the material as a result of their subjective choices. Moreover, thematic, archetypal material seemed irrelevant to them. From their point of view, what I brought up was simply a foolish possibility.

Yet the whole problem of complete objectivity for the serious biographer still remains a central issue. For instance, I talked with Sir Philip Magnus, author of lives of Burke, of Kitchener, and lately of King Edward VII. When I asked him if he thought biographers were ever aware of the real reasons for various choices which they had to make, he replied that he doubted it. Not many writers, he insisted, were wholly conscious of what they were doing and why. He thought most of them worked largely through a series of intuitions or hunches. He doubted that any biographer could ever say just why he made any particular choice. It merely seemed the logical thing to do at the time.

Magnus said that his theory of biography was to present all the essential facts with no comment. The biographer, he thought, should not enter the picture. He must retain a "dead-pan" attitude, from a detached, lofty position. One can include any kind of nasty detail, Magnus said, if it is introduced with dignity. What causes trouble is sniggering or prurience on the part of the biographers.

When I pointed out to him that many of the reviewers of his life of Kitchener had noted the unfavorable part of his portrait and ignored the attractive, which would seem to indicate that his attempt to follow this procedure had not worked completely, he kept on insisting that he had never tried to attack Kitchener. But he did admit that as he did research for the life his dislike of certain aspects of Kitchener's character had increased. He had started out with great enthusiasm, even with sympathy for the colonial stance of his subject, but gradually, as he amassed the evidence, he found that sympathy dwindling. Yet he still thought he had produced a fair picture of the man.

But it surely is significant that many readers clearly sensed his inherent dislike of Kitchener, no matter how carefully he tried to be fair. Obviously the writer's true feelings cannot be wholly hidden. The book was clearly Magnus on Kitchener, revealing in devious ways his own ambivalent attitudes towards his subject.

At Oxford I had a delightful visit with Lord David Cecil, who is an animated talker. As he spoke, the words seemed to be tumbling out, and often he could hardly keep up with himself. We talked about his well-known biographies—the superbly written study of Lord Melbourne, the account of Cowper in *The Stricken Deer*, and the study of Gray. At that time he was just beginning to work on Max Beerbohm, and was uncertain as to what approach to make. To digress a moment, I might cite this as one example of how a biographer sometimes changes his mind completely as he assembles his material. When I talked to Lord David in 1959 he told me that he had been chosen by Beerbohm to be his official biographer because Beerbohm knew that he would do a short, condensed, artistic portrait. This was what he wanted. But in 1964, when the book finally came out, it had been expanded to over five hundred pages, and contained all sorts of miscellaneous information. It showed little of the compressed evaluation which Beerbohm had desired. Something had happened in the process of writing, which even Lord David might find it difficult to explain.

One point Lord David made clear at the start—that he could never write a biography about anyone unless he had some emotional or intellectual tie to the man. Somehow, he had to be involved, even before he began to collect evidence. There must be some strong connection—family, social background, or mental sympathy. Melbourne had been a relative, Gray was a cloistered academic scholar, and with Cowper the psychological troubles were what had fascinated him. Indeed, at every point Lord David kept insisting on his own personal involvement throughout the whole process.

When I brought up my basic question as to whether, as he wrote, he was aware of the nature of the decisions he was making, he said "No." He never asked himself "Why am I choosing this bit of evidence instead of another?" He thought most of his decisions had been intuitive. He "felt" this was right and that was not. He thought he worked wholly through intuition. Although he tried hard to analyze the evidence historically, the actual composition was like writing a novel. He obviously thought of himself as a creative writer.

Let me cite one more illustration of what I might call the creative biographer—this time Elizabeth Jenkins, whose very popular life of Queen Elizabeth I was the choice of the Book-of-the-Month Club. We had lunch one day near the British Museum, and discussed the way she worked. As she put it, what she wanted to do was to give a credible picture of her subject, stressing the little human details which the historians tend to leave out. She even admitted to taking a feminine point of view.

When I asked Miss Jenkins whether she thought much about form and organization of material, or about the technique of life-writing, she said emphatically that she had not. Her chief aim was to tell a smooth story. She did not even plan divisions or chapters beforehand. They just developed. She would start writing, and when she came to a place where there seemed to be a break, she stopped the chapter. As soon as she began composition, she felt almost as if she were in a trance, as if the story were telling itself. It came to her without effort.

Even so, I asked her the same old question: did she consciously try to be objective in her choices of material, or realize ever that she was exerting subjective judgment? She seemed puzzled, and insisted such an idea had never crossed her mind. She knew intuitively what was coming next. Even when searching for material in the State Papers or in other historical repositories, she would sometimes have a queer feeling that on the next page she would find something important, and usually there it would be. Of course, she had become so obsessed by her subject and felt that she knew her inside out, that the story seemed to write itself.

I had two very pleasant discussions with Sir Harold Nicolson, covering the whole range of biographical theory and practice. As the author of a number of biographies and an excellent short history of the genre, Nicolson was deeply involved. At the first meeting we were joined for lunch by Raymond Mortimer, who also had decided views on the subject. Both kept insisting on the necessity of emotional involvement on the part of the biographer. As Mortimer put it, one should not write a life unless he was much attracted to or hated his subject deeply. If he were only mildly interested it would be better to do something else. We argued at length about this point, particularly the possibility of hate being a proper motivating factor. They both cited Strachey as an example of a man who detested some of his subjects, yet produced remarkable studies. When I kept insisting that either complete love or hate on the part of the author was certain to distort a life, and suggested that a kind of sympathetic involvement or a passionate curiosity might be a more useful approach, they partially agreed, but still defended their belief in the necessity for strong emotional commitment on the part of the biographer.

At the same time, Sir Harold did admit that too strong an aversion might well ruin a work, and gave as an example the fact that once he had considered writing a life of Alexander Pope, whose poetry he greatly admired, but found that he disliked him too much. He simply could not go on with the project. The traditional nineteenth-century view of Pope as a nasty person was still too strong in his mind. Nicolson also admitted that he had years ago started work on a life of Anselm, whom he thought a fascinating character. In this instance he gave up because of lack of facility with the medieval background. Knowledge of the times is sometimes as essential as involvement with character.

As active critics, both Nicolson and Mortimer agreed that they had no doubt about the importance of a subtle interaction between author and subject when it came to fashioning a life, particularly in the area of choice of material. Yet they, too, were convinced that not many practicing biographers were completely aware of just what they were doing.

As an example of the way a writer selects material to produce the character he wishes to project, Sir Harold cited Leonard Woolf and his protective presentation of his wife, Virginia, since her death. In the excerpts he published from her diary and in what he allowed to be printed from other sources the character which emerges is that of a distraught, doomed, and rather morbid person, who needed his strength and protection. Undoubtedly Leonard Woolf was not himself fully aware of what he was doing, that he was in a way attempting to shape her personality for posterity. Lady Nicolson, Sir Harold added, had a marvelous series of letters from Virginia, but Leonard would not allow them to be published. They showed Virginia in her lighter moments, more frivolous, more the writer of *Mrs. Dalloway*, than that of the diary—at least of those parts that have so far appeared. Sir Harold further cited the fact that when his two boys were in their teens, and he would remark that Virginia Woolf was coming to lunch, they would shout with joy. She was a great favorite with them because she was so much fun.

I casually asked about *Orlando*, assuming it was a kind of biography of Lady Nicolson, though in jumbled time sequence, and citing Leon Edel's remarks about it in his Alexander lectures.[2] Sir Harold corrected me and said it was a portrait. In one of Virginia's letters to Lady Nicolson she commented that she had finished some work or other, and was beginning a biography to be called "Orlando," or something like that. "Did Lady Nicolson know what she was doing?" I asked. He laughed and said that she suspected something, for Virginia was taking so many pictures of her.

When I kept returning to my chief point—the question of whether a reader can evaluate properly the involvement of the author in shaping a character, Sir Harold admitted that he knew of no useful rules to recommend. As he put it, the basic psychology of biography—that is, the inner motivations of the biographer and how they affect the resulting life—is largely unexplored territory. He very much wished to see more written on the subject.

ঽ৶

Any number of instances could be cited to show how a biographer's own inner convictions are unconsciously grafted on his subject. In his life of Milton in the *Lives of the Poets*, written in the late 1770's, Dr. Johnson refers to Milton's continued failure to reform in the matter of holding family prayer, and he comments: "The neglect of it in his family was probably a fault for which he condemned himself, and which he intended to correct, but that death, as too often happens, intercepted his reformation."[3] Here the author has undoubtedly attributed his own feelings to Milton, for Johnson's prayers and meditations are filled with just this sort of self-castigation. But from what is known of Milton's character it is highly unlikely that he would have followed such a course. There is little genuine evidence as to Milton's failure to reform and his subsequent unhappiness.

Lytton Strachey in his *Queen Victoria* says that Albert had a "marked distaste for the opposite sex" and was really never in love with Victoria. But it is an interpretation based on very little evidence. Now Michael Holroyd in his life of Strachey suggests that this remark about Albert's dislike of women may have been caused by Strachey's reading something of himself into the character of Albert. In view of the homosexual orientation of Strachey which Holroyd clearly shows, this explanation seems convincing.[4]

Any choice of external evidence to be used is inevitably dependent upon the author's personal approach. Consider this hypothetical case. Suppose a biographer has discovered a hundred letters from X to Y, covering a decade or so, not one of the most interesting and productive periods of X's life. The biographer has decided that he can allot only a small space in his book to this sterile period, and so is faced with the task of selecting merely a phrase or two, here and there, from these hundred letters. Consequently he goes through the correspondence picking out what he wants to use. But why does he choose one sentence rather than another? What motives are behind each choice? Does he know himself?

Or if the biographer has discovered a full diary kept by Z, one of X's good friends, in which there are many accounts of pleasant meetings and bitter quarrels, some sentimentally affectionate, and others openly critical, how should the author use the material? Some selection is required, for he cannot quote all of the entries. Should the bland, favorable reactions be stressed? Or the bitter, jaundiced attacks? If an even balance is attempted, will this actually give a wrong impression? Is there any way to guess the reasons behind Z's changeable behavior? Somehow the biographer will have to decide what it all meant, and thus in the end there must be a subjective evaluation of the evidence.

Obviously each choice is subtly tied to the biographer's own feelings and loyalties. Take Gertrude Himmelfarb's recent volume, *Victorian Minds*, where Miss Himmelfarb examines the traditional characterizations of a number of well-known nineteenth-century figures. She clearly shows, by the selection of details usually ignored in earlier studies, how quite different portraits can be created. The evidence is just as authentic; it is merely a matter of what is used. Earlier biographers molded their studies to fit the conventional image. A twentieth-century writer who independently chooses from the same mass of genuine evidence may come up with a very different character.

Sometimes the selection of evidence is dependent on the sensibility of the age in which the writer is working. Marchette Chute gives as an example the relationship of Shakespeare to various noblemen, notably the Earl of Southampton and the Earl of Pembroke. Actually there is very little factual evidence linking Shakespeare to these men, nothing to connect him to them personally during a fifteen-year period. But nineteenth-century biographers who were convinced that few things were as important as an English Lord, or as unimportant as an actor, kept guessing that Shakespeare's genius must have been due to his association with noblemen. "Basking in their exalted company" gave him inspiration for his plays.[5]

At times the sex of the biographer influences his interpretation of the evidence. An amusing example is Froude's thesis that Jane Carlyle was a sensitive, misunderstood woman, almost like an unhappy servant under the selfish domination of her unfeeling husband. Yet Elizabeth Drew in her study of Jane pictures Carlyle as a gentle and loyal husband, not upset by Jane's continual complaints. Here are two opposite theses, each one based on dependable evidence, using extracts from genuine letters, correctly quoted. Each by itself is entirely convincing. As has been suggested, Froude obviously fell in love with his heroine; while Miss Drew was sympathetically drawn to Carlyle.[6]

Edgar Johnson called my attention to another example. When Sir Herbert Grierson was preparing his twelve-volume edition of Sir Walter Scott's letters, he had access to great masses of Scott material in the possession of the Duke of Buccleuch. As he read through the collection, Grierson decided that most of the letters were uninteresting, concerned with "local doings in politics, electioneering, and jobbery," and so in his edition he omitted long passages from the correspondence.[7] When Edgar Johnson finally saw the original letters he thought them fascinating and very important. He was looking for different kinds of evidence, and in the passages omitted by Grierson he found just what he wanted.

As I keep reiterating, the conviction held by some historians of the possibility of complete objectivity in the selection of evidence is an illusion. Every re-creation of character represents subjective judgment on the part of the creator, and this is good. Noel Annan admirably sums it up: "A biographer has to take a view of what his hero was really like, or what sort of a man he became at different times in his life, and then the biographer has to manipulate his material to sustain that view. If he does not do this, his book becomes a collection of lumps of undigested material or is a dreary mausoleum."[8]

Again I come back to the valuable talk I had with Edgar Johnson.

When faced with the crucial problem of how a biographer chooses quotations or pieces of evidence, Johnson admitted that, as something of a theorist himself on the art of biography, he had thought deeply on the subject. He knew that most biographers, including himself, started with some well-developed idea of what his subject had been like, and inevitably chose his evidence to support this pattern. He saw no possible way that this could be avoided. What is important is to make every effort to keep an open mind, ready to make changes whenever necessary.

He was quite aware of the dangers of subjective evaluation of evidence. Improperly used it can produce warped, fallacious characterizations. Even with honest, well-intentioned biographers there are unconscious motivations to contend with. He reminded me of what Charles Darwin once said, that whenever he came across anything with which he violently disagreed he made a note of it, for otherwise he would forget it. There is often an automatic blocking out in the mind of disagreeable facts. The biographer tends to remember details which fit his pattern and to forget those which do not. Thus to be sure of a balanced view, he should make notes of such details as he goes along.

There is always the temptation, too, to see beneath the surface more than is really there. In a very shrewd analysis Marchette Chute has pointed out the dangers of our modern passion for pattern-making by describing a typical hypothetical case.[9] After years of persistent effort, a biographer thinks he sees various pieces of evidence fall into place. As he plays with various items like a jigsaw puzzle, A, B, and D appear to fit together in a recognizable pattern. Eagerly he searches for C, which will complete the design. Suddenly something turns up which at first glance looks like C. With a little trimming of the edges and some juggling, it might be made to fit into the pattern. The temptation to think the matter settled becomes overpowering. At that moment, says Miss Chute, the biographer must take a deep breath and put his neat pattern aside, at least for the moment. He must always remember that the real C may be discovered later. Or his analysis of the relationship of A, B, and D may have been wrong. He must firmly take himself in hand and resist the desire to impose a pattern. The trouble is that the author is usually unaware that he is forcing the evidence, that his own subconscious desires are what have been pushing him in this direction.

To return, then, to the question posed at the beginning of the chapter—how does a biographer choose his evidence? Eternal vigilance is the answer, and at the same time a recognition that the whole process is basically subjective. If biography is, as Edgar Johnson puts it, "a psychological intersection between the personality of the biographer and that of his subject," then the ways of the writer must be intricate and subtle. No simple rules will suffice. And if this is so, the general reader, who wishes to evaluate the truth which lies behind the finished work in his hands, may have an even more difficult time.

9. How Much Should a Biographer Tell? ๙

Today the most difficult problem facing a biographer is not so much selecting a proper form or validating evidence and estimating its relevance, but deciding how much of all the available material to use. The term "how much," of course, can have different meanings. It can be merely quantitative, referring to the number of details to include about everyday affairs. Or it can refer to ethical considerations—the question of how deeply to go into another person's private life or how much to reveal concerning his contemporaries. In our post-Freudian era there is the added complication of deciding whether to attempt psychological explanations.

As I have shown elsewhere in some detail,[1] these matters were rarely discussed until the late eighteenth-century. Earlier critics were not interested since biography was hardly considered a literary genre. In classical times, if thought of at all, it was a minor tool for historical writing. No effort was made to analyze the structural or ethical problems of life-writing. During the Middle Ages, when biography was largely devoted to saints' lives, there were no significant analyses of hagiography, or at least no attempts to define or describe this method of writing, or to examine the psychological questions faced by a man who was writing about a saint.[2] Even throughout the Renaissance and seventeenth centuries there were no separate critical discussions of biography. Everyone still assumed that the writer of a life knew what to do—he merely gathered the facts and strung what he wanted of them together in a chronological account. In fact the only choice he had was whether to write a eulogy or a savage attack. There appears to have been no arguing over how to present a three-dimensional life.

What is still a bit shocking to me is the fact that in the first half of the eighteenth century, when thousands of periodical essays were appearing on all sorts of topics, there is not a single entire essay on biography or the problems of a biographer. Apparently there was no real curiosity (except for Roger North, who kept his speculations to himself) and no significant difference of opinion strong enough to elicit critical discussion, until the middle of the eighteenth century. Samuel Johnson's *Rambler* No. 60, in 1750, is almost the first full treatment, and even Johnson does not probe very deeply. To be sure, in his conversations with Boswell, Johnson shows some awareness of some of the difficulties. He wonders whether Addison's heavy drinking should have been made public, but he seems to have vacillated between an insistence on telling the whole truth, and the necessity of protecting the sensibilities of a man's family and friends.

Not until the furor following Boswell's revealing accounts of Johnson's own private conversations was the general public awakened to the possibilities of the new biography. At last life-writing came to the center of the stage. Sometimes it is forgotten that Boswell was subjected to the same kind of vituperation that has fallen on sensational practitioners in our time. Boswell's insistence on giving the whole story, or at least most of what he knew about it, clearly represented a new approach to contemporary life-writing. Everyone who followed was forced to consider at least the possibility of rivaling Boswell's comprehensive coverage. The modern world of biography, then, is post-Boswell.

Some readers may object that I am forgetting classical biographers like Suetonius, who possibly accumulated huge masses of evidence for his accounts of the Roman emperors. He might even have kept a diary, as did Boswell, verifying his discoveries with care. My point is that there is no surviving evidence to support such a guess. It is impossible for us to know how Suetonius worked, or whether he had proper checks and balances. If ever there were contemporary arguments of the sort we now engage in, the evidence has long since disappeared. I still claim that not until the time of Boswell, when competent authorities openly disagreed, was there sufficient public discussion to produce a viable issue. Nearly two centuries after Boswell certain nagging questions still remain to be answered.

First, however, it may be well to examine the quantitative approach. How many irrelevant details will readers plow through without protesting? Take the question of the size of Lord Nelson's head and his eyeshade mentioned earlier. Was Oliver Warner's curiosity as to these matters legitimate? And once he had found Nelson's measurements, should he burden his readers with such trivialities? When a biographer is describing an important meeting of his subject with a close friend, is it advisable to tell just what they had to eat, assuming that the biographer has discovered the bill of fare? Which facts are really significant, and which are not?

Obviously much depends upon what kind of biography is intended—whether a short, interpretative study, or a many-volumed life and works. For a brief character sketch details must be kept at a minimum, while a lengthy work has room for more. The question of how much to include is important, and at least since the middle of the eighteenth century has been the source of continuous argument, often with open and violent disagreement.

In 1758 Owen Ruffhead, when reviewing Jortin's *Life of Erasmus* in the *Monthly Review*, had some caustic allusions to the many "laborious drones," without genius, taste, or learning, who merely collect materials and put them together without discrimination or judgment.

These industrious drudges, equal to any fatigue themselves, seem to imagine that their readers can never be tired. Their writings are like old women's stories, in which we do not lose a single *How d'ye do?* They, no doubt, think it the office of a faithful historian, not to omit the most trivial anecdote; and they often insult our patience with tedious relations, as uninteresting as if they were to acquaint us—That on such an hour, of such a day, in such a year, the Hero of their endless tale sat down to pair his nails.[3]

Late in the century the biographer's piling up of insignificant details became a popular theme for the satirists. William Beckford's youthful burlesque entitled *Biographical Memoirs of Extraordinary Painters*, published in 1780 when he was nineteen, is one example[4] and John Wolcot's hilarious take-offs of Boswell and Mrs. Piozzi were unmerciful. Under the pen name of Peter Pindar, Wolcot pounced on Boswell's *Tour to the Hebrides*, pointing out the mass of inconsequential trivial material which was included in the journal. A "curious Scrapmonger," he calls Boswell—a purveyor of foolish anecdotes.

> How are we all with rapture touched to see
> Where, when, and at what hour, you swallowed Tea;
> How once, to grace this Asiatic treat,
> Came Haddocks, which the Rambler could not eat!
> . . . .
> Oh! while amid the Anecdotic mine
> Thou labour'st hard to bid thy Hero shine,
> Run to Bolt Court, exert thy Curll-like soul,
> And fish for *golden* leaves from hole to hole:
> Find when he ate and drank, cough'd and sneezed;
> Let all his *motions* in thy Book be squeezed:
> On tales, however strange, impose thy claw;
> Yes, let thy Amber lick up every Straw:
> Sam's nods, and winks, and laughs, will form a treat;
> For *all* that breathes of Johnson *must* be *great*.[5]

Yet in contrast, many contemporary readers of Boswell delighted in the wealth of detail. Ralph Griffiths, reviewing the *Life of Johnson* in the *Monthly Review*, insisted that he would urge the reporter to "Give us *all*; suppress nothing; lest in rejecting that which, in your estimation may seem to be of inferior value, you unwarily throw away gold with the dross."[6] Boswell, Griffith maintained, had not "set before us too plenteous an entertainment."

In our day there is the same split—some readers complaining about too much trivial evidence, others eagerly asking for the fullest coverage. Let me quote from a few reviews of recent volumes on modern literary figures. Each admittedly is a major contribution to knowledge, and each has had its share of encomiums. But here are some of the critics' objections. Mark Schorer in his *Sinclair Lewis* (1961), has presented his subject "utterly befeathered in facts."[7] Had he "spared us the tedium of so much of Lewis's daily life, had he cut his book by half," Schorer might have shown Lewis as he really was. "Mr. Schorer is the victim of the exhaustive fallacy in biography." The first volume of Michael Holroyd's challenging life of Strachey (1967) is "boring" because he "reproduces every inconsequential letter in full, though one Strachey letter is very much like another."[8] John Unterecker, author of *Voyager: A Life of Hart Crane* (1969) is criticized for being "unable to present what is typical and let the rest go." And the reviewer continues, "surely there must be many people who are fed up as I am with nonwriting, the unselective, repetitive chronicling of trivia that you meet with in so-called biographies."[9] Similarly Leon Edel, whose work on Henry James has already been fully discussed, is attacked for omitting nothing—"neither the Master's feeblest witticism about Italian pastry nor his refusal of the vice-presidency of the Rye cricket-club."[10] The same kind of objections have been leveled at other full-scale biographies such as Carlos Baker's *Hemingway*.

On the other hand, many modern biographers and critics are convinced that small details, if skillfully handled, are vital for the creation of color and the semblance of reality. Brilliant Stracheyan summations are not enough. In my talks with Edgar Johnson he kept coming back to what he called the necessity for "density." It was, he said, one of his chief concerns. Of crucial importance, he insisted, is the amount of matter—one might even say peripheral matter—which can be brought in to create the illusion of real life. In general, he claimed, he was on the side of fullness. He believed in bringing in enough vivid descriptive touches so that the reader can feel that he is actually living with the subject. Even some apparently inconsequential material may be needed to provide richness for the background. Without resorting to any fictional devices or overloading the backdrop, it is important, in his opinion, to describe everything surrounding the subject with as much detail as possible.

But who decides what is possible? Is it the author or the reader? Must there be some kind of testing along the way? And does the decision largely depend on how skillfully the biographer is able to hide his triviality? Undoubtedly, there must be a place where everyone agrees that too much is too much. But finding that exact point is a delicate, often perplexing matter. One critic thinks that there are too many little details; another wishes for more. The worried biographer, who must somehow make the final decision, is caught between, and inevitably must be willing to accept some stringent criticism from those who disagree.

There are, of course, various paths to follow for the scrupulous author who has in his files masses of evidence concerned directly with his subject, and yet who would like to save the reader from boredom. He certainly does not have to print it all, at least not in the main fabric of the life. He can put extra facts in an appendix, where the reader can ignore them if he wishes. Or he can put many of them in a long note. Or even better the material can be published separately in a long article in a scholarly journal or *Festschrift*. Frederick Pottle was able to discover a great deal concerning Boswell's university education—the teachers he had, the texts he used, and the lectures he attended—which he put together in a learned essay for a volume in honor of L. F. Powell of Oxford.[11] As a result, in the first volume of his admirable life of Boswell he was able to skim quickly over the period, touching only the high spots, and referring the curious reader to his assembling of all the details elsewhere.

Total volume is one problem; relevance is another. Although often the problems are closely related, sometimes they are not. As I pointed out earlier, there are times when evidence is so scarce that anything, no matter how irrelevant, must be included. It might be exciting to find out definitely whether Shakespeare preferred beef or mutton. On the other hand, it seems obvious that where there is an abundance of material, the biographer must carefully consider each decision, making certain that if a seemingly minor point is included it is for some good reason, whether structural or critical. To pile up details, merely to show off the scholar's skill in research, or to cover up a lack of understanding of character, is always dangerous. Critics have an uncanny way of spotting such deficiencies.

The second, and even more controversial, problem in making a choice of evidence is ethical. What kinds of personal details can be given to the public without offending family and friends? What secrets can be revealed? Are there private matters which must never be told? Or is it a question of timing? If one waits until all the subject's family and friends are dead, can everything be safely told? If not, how much longer must one wait? A hundred years? Less than that? Alas! These are not questions which can be easily or quickly answered.

Even though Boswell did not tell everything he knew about Johnson, to many readers of his biography it seemed a shocking invasion of privacy. "Would any man," commented Mrs. Montagu, so-called Queen of the Bluestockings, "who wish'd his friend to have the respect of posterity exhibit all his little caprices, his unhappy infirmities, his singularities?"[12] "This new-fashioned biography," Hannah More wrote to her sister, "seems to value itself upon perpetuating every thing that is injurious and detracting."[13] And Dr. Burney, in the *Monthly Review* minced no words in his expression of disapproval. After citing Cicero's diatribe against Anthony for revealing matters told in secret, he continued: "What admirer of the moral excellencies, and of the extensive learning of the late Samuel Johnson, can forbear feeling the same indignation, and expressing it with equal warmth, when they behold his former friends exposing his failings and his weaknesses, to the curious, yet fastidious eye of the Public."[14] As Bishop Percy, some years later, summed up the conservative attitude: "It is surely an exception more than venial to violate one of the first and most sacred laws of society, by publishing private and unguarded conversation of unsuspecting company into which he was accidentally admitted."[15]

In the century that followed, Victorian reticence kept discussion of the issue of invasion of privacy at a minimum, since few biographers were willing to court public displeasure by revealing their subjects' private lives. Lockhart, while he had learned much from Boswell, resolutely refused to report casual talk in his life of Scott.[16] But with the twentieth century, and the rebirth of debunking techniques, the question has again loomed large. Modern critics find it one of the most difficult and perplexing of problems. Yet even in our day there is no apparent consensus as to what can be told. Again and again the question is asked as to how much should be told about the disagreeable or nasty episodes in a man's life. Boswell has claimed that he was presenting Johnson "warts and all," but, as Stephen Spender acutely points out, "warts are not the same as intestines."[17]

It is all very well to describe a man's bad temper, or his silly foibles, or to point out that occasionally he drank too much, but what about secret love affairs, illegitimate children, or the subject's syphilis? Or that he had been a very clever thief, who fooled all his reputable friends, while at the same time he was in the forefront of liberal causes? One may answer, "It all depends. . . ." But on what?

Even when the revelations are not too shocking, there is still the question of whether casual conversation involving other people can be published. Does the biographer have to secure the consent of everyone mentioned before anything is revealed? One recent critical flurry may serve as a good example by which to set up the basic themes.

I refer to the uproar in England which followed the publication of Lord Moran's *Winston Churchill: The Struggle for Survival* (1966). It must at once be admitted that the whole argument was complicated by the fact that Lord Moran had been Churchill's personal physician. As I have already pointed out in Chapter 5, the question of whether a professional man can ever pass on information received from a client is a prickly one. That a doctor should reveal details and confidences of the sickroom shocked many people. Statesmen, generals, even secretaries are permitted to make public their recollections about other people, but not medical men. By the rules of their profession doctors, lawyers, and priests are not supposed to tell what they know. "The secrets of the sick room," one noble lord protested, "should be almost as closely guarded as those of the confessional."[18] The volume, another complained, constituted "a grave violation of the ethical code."[19] And many others agreed. As a result, Lord Moran was publicly censured by the British Medical Association.

As might have been expected, Lord Moran defended himself with vigor. Accepting the fact that a doctor's obligation to secrecy "is absolute in the lifetime of a patient," he nevertheless insisted that it is not applicable to a great historical figure, such as Sir Winston Churchill, after his death, since it is inevitable that his illnesses will be described in detail by the laity.

The lay accounts seldom pretend to accuracy. It seems to me that any doctor involved is entitled to correct such inaccuracies and, if they appear to criticize his conduct of the case, to present his defence. . . . It is not possible to follow the last 25 years of Sir Winston's life without a knowledge of his medical background. It was exhaustion of mind and body that accounted for much that is otherwise inexplicable. . . . Only a doctor can give the facts accurately.[20]

The medical angle, however, is only one part of the larger question with which we are dealing. In addition to describing at great length the various symptoms which appeared during Churchill's illnesses, Lord Moran repeats casual conversations on a variety of other topics, without asking the permission of those who were quoted. The result was an outburst of protests to the newspapers— letters implying that the published versions were not accurate, cries of anger over the making public of remarks heard in private conversation. One associate of Lord Moran complained, "Lord Moran asked me these questions in his professional capacity as Sir Winston's doctor. It was natural for me to assume, as I certainly did, that he was putting them to me in confidence."[21] Another commented, "The wholesale reporting of private conversations transgresses the canons of good manners." If such reporting without permission continues, he added, "the private life of public men will become intolerable, and only Trappists will hold high office of state with equanimity."[22]

Not that Lord Moran was without defenders. "I have found nothing in his book which in any way offends good taste or propriety. Sir Winston Churchill emerges an even greater man than we knew before, greater because more human," wrote one correspondent to the London *Times*.[23] "There is some advantage in publishing records of this kind while some of the people are alive and can answer as they think fit. If publication is delayed till everyone concerned is dead, historical criticism is much more difficult," added Denis Brogan a few days later.[24] And Malcolm Elwin thus summed up his opinion: "Lord Moran was obviously faced with a painfully difficult decision, and should surely be congratulated on risking the condemnation of conventional opinion in the interest of historical truth."[25]

Throughout the whole heated argument one point was often stressed—the resemblance to Boswell. One reviewer after another made the comparison: "He was more than Churchill's physician. He was Churchill's Boswell." "Meanwhile, rightly or wrongly, here is a sustained attempt to Boswellize Churchill." "Perhaps without fully realizing it, Lord Moran has been more Boswell than physician." "His diary betrays the self-conscious Boswell. In particular, he reproduces dialogue with apparent fidelity, and he has a sharp eye for the little things which make a scene and a person live."[26]

Whether by design or accident, Lord Moran's procedure was very similar to that of his eighteenth-century predecessor. He jotted down short notes on his way back from meetings with his subject, on backs of envelopes and scraps of paper, and then wrote them up in fuller form soon afterward. His book was, in the main, produced from these day-by-day accounts with little revision. And so we have, almost two hundred years apart, two devoted biographers, setting down notes of actual conversations with important people, and publishing them uncensored by those involved. Human nature being what it is, the resulting furor has been almost identical. It is the same old problem. But to say this provides little practical help for the worried author, trying to decide what he ought to do.

In an earlier discussion I came to the rather discouraging conclusion that there was no middle way, that for a biographer approaching a contemporary subject the choice lay between keeping on good terms with all of his friends and relations and thus disappointing posterity, or of taking the harder approach of braving the displeasure of his own day with the hope of eventual recognition in the future.[27] I still think that basically this is the choice. But a leader-writer in the *Times Literary Supplement* suggests that I was being too partisan, and was judging chiefly from the side of the biographer. I had not sufficiently explored the rights of other people.

It is certainly not the case—confidence being a two-sided thing—that every seal of confidence placed by a man during his lifetime expires with his death. Many undoubtedly do, including most of those he, like all of us, has imposed solely in his own interest and for the sake of his own good name. But some seals are not set entirely for these reasons. They may have been imposed, wholly or mainly, for the benefits of others: for example, a decision not to tell a son the true particulars of his birth. In such cases, while it might be for others, it is hardly for the biographer to question the dead man's judgment and expose the secret. The important thing is that each life is part of a tissue of confidences which extend to many lives, and it is only when all those lives have ceased that some degree of ethical obligation to maintain the confidence finally vanishes. The biographer has at any rate an obligation to consider the motives which caused his subject to keep something quiet, and to give some measure of respect to those motives which regard others.[28]

In other words, there are both selfish and generous motives behind secrecy, and it is up to the writer of a life to respect the latter, if not the former.

The *TLS* critic sees clearly that if this doctrine were pushed to extremities there would be grave losses to literature and history. The Boswells and the Lord Morans are the ones who best succeed in making their subjects live for future ages. Their method of privately writing down all they can pick up during their subject's lifetime is probably the only way to obtain the "living truth about a great man." But it is equally true that it is unethical for a biographer to allow himself to "be the agent of posthumous vindictiveness," or to glory in piercing all the reticences and secrets of his subject and his family.

To this I heartily agree, but still think the final decision must be centered on the question of historical truth. It is all very well to protect other people's feelings, though not if it means any real distortion of history. Everything still depends on the biographer's conception of his duty to posterity.

Nevertheless, I am wholly in accord with the suggestion that what must be considered first are the subject's own reasons for secrecy. In each instance the biographer must ask himself if there is any way of determining the basic motives behind this bit of reticence, or that carefully buried secret. Was what was hidden really disreputable, or merely some little personal vanity? Did it seriously involve other living persons? If so, how materially would they be hurt if the secret were known? The author must try to find out why other people might prefer not to have their casual conversations made public—whether because they later changed their position, or because the remarks were indiscreet or had been carelessly phrased and lacked style. Or was it merely from a determination to avoid any kind of publicity whatsoever?

These are only a few of the questions which the biographer should ask himself. Not that he can always be sure that he has conclusive answers. No one can ever succeed in getting inside the mind of another person, though sometimes it is possible, with the help of other evidence, to speculate with comparative certainty.

Once he has decided on the motives behind the covering up of evidence in the past—whether the result of conscious censorship on the part of his subject, or merely reticence concerning personal matters—then what does the biographer do? Perhaps the only answer would be that he must somehow establish a series of categories, ranging from over-sensitivity to publicity or foolish prudery, to other more justifiable motives. His task, then, and it will not be an easy one, is to try to determine by this scale what he must omit or include.

If a man was averse to letting anyone know that he was bald and wore a toupee, or that he had false teeth, these are forgivable vanities, but such reticence need not bind a later biographer, provided there is some value in mentioning such little details. In another category might be the fact that the man was very miserly and refused to contribute to worthy causes, or that he was vindictive in his treatment of underlings. In still another category might be his amorous indiscretions. Going even farther, as the *TLS* writer suggested, there might be the proof that he had sired an illegitimate son, still living yet unaware of his paternity. In the latter instance almost everyone would agree that the biographer should allow this secret to remain hidden, though at the same time not destroying the evidence but putting it away somewhere for future biographers.

Or consider the case of the Victorian Prime Minister William

Gladstone, whose efforts to rescue poor girls who had become prostitutes brought him at times dangerously near scandal.[29] Obviously what he was doing, even though his motives were completely honorable, could easily be misconstrued. Thus after his death a biographer would have been completely justified in making clear exactly what he did, and his family should not have tried to keep it secret. Since rumors were sure to grow, it would have been, in this instance, better for Gladstone's reputation that all the facts be available immediately and not only some wild guesses.

I have here been merely setting up a few different categories which seem to me to demand varying treatment. When carefully hidden details are the issue, then the value to the reader, or to the subject himself, must be balanced against the anguish to others. Yet the whole procedure is more complicated than it may appear, even the handling of inconsequential details like wearing a toupee. Although some readers might claim that such personal idiosyncracies are irrelevant, it is quite possible that when vanity is a central theme in a man's life it is important to assemble all available examples to prove the point. The toupee might even be shown to be a dramatic symbol of a fundamental weakness in the man's character. As another example, if his sexual license seriously affected his relations with his wife, or children, the details of his affairs may have central relevance. If they cannot be documented without causing much unhappiness to others, they may at least be hinted at. To put it another way, if what is hidden shows the subject to be very different from his professed character or conventional image, then the importance of truth may override any obligations of confidence. Each matter must be judged on its own merits. What is vital is that it be judged fairly, and that there be a balancing of pressures and contingencies.

Unfortunately not many practicing biographers will be willing to spend the time required for this kind of evaluation of each separate piece of evidence. Obviously this would be asking too much. But if writers were constantly aware of the problem and kept at the back of their minds some kind of evaluation system which would balance considerations of relevance and ethics, of historical truth and private anguish, then, as they work, material might fall more easily into place. Such a procedure, of course, is what the *TLS* writer is suggesting and what most of us would eagerly desire.

ૐ

Equally perplexing, though in another way, is the problem of whether a biographer is justified in searching for patterns of behavior, or whether he can effectively "psychoanalyze" a person whom he has never met. An entire book could be written on that question alone. Often the temptation is great, when Freudian symbols seem to pop up constantly. But every time I have tentatively posed the question to some practicing psychiatrist I have been greeted with tolerant laughter. The usual answer is that it is difficult enough to get at the truth when we have a patient on the couch before us, willing to talk for years on end. How can anyone expect to find anything dependable from a few incidental references in letters or diaries, when there is no opportunity to go deeply into hidden motives?

Yet many biographers have been loath to accept such a blanket rebuff, and in the 1920's and 1930's there were numerous attempts to apply Freudian theories. Among the earliest were Katharine Anthony's *Margaret Fuller* (1920), and Joseph Wood Krutch's study of Edgar Allan Poe (1926), which Krutch would be the first to admit was a bit oversimplified. Both appeared in the vanguard of the new approach. Lewis Mumford's *Herman Melville* (1929) and L. P. Clark's *Lincoln* (1933) could be named as other examples, and Erik H. Erikson's studies of Luther and Ghandi show the technique at its best.[30]

It might be stressed that the alternative for a life-writer is neither total acceptance of Freudian or Jungian theories, nor complete rejection. Even for those who rule out technical analysis there is still the possibility of being acutely aware of psychological themes and patterns as they may appear. While he moves along he can keep his eyes open for significant clues. Moreover, there are different degrees of endorsement.

Richard Ellmann's *The Identity of Yeats* (1954) is an example of a fairly dogmatic acceptance of the importance of symbols in a writer's life and works, where the author assumes that he has discovered the truth and passes it along to the reader with few qualifications. Many other recent writers have elected that approach.

A persuasive defense of the use of Freudian psychology in biography comes from Leon Edel. In his admirable Alexander Lectures, published as *Literary Biography* (1957; enlarged ed. 1959), and in other essays, he shows what he thinks can and cannot be done with this technique.[31] Although he sees clearly all the dangers involved, Edel suggests that "the answer to the misguided use of psychoanalysis is not to close our ears but to ask ourselves: how are we to handle this difficult material while remaining true to our own disciplines—and avoid making complete fools of ourselves?"[32] His point is that we must try to master the new techniques and then try to adapt them to our own.

Our success will depend entirely on the extent to which we know what we are about and the way in which we use these shiny new tools. We must not run amuck; above all we must beware of the terminology and jargon of the psycho-analysts. What we must try to do is to translate the terms in a meaningful way and into language proper to ourselves. Critics who babble of the Oedipus complex and who plant psycho-analytical clichés higgledy-piggledy in their writings do a disservice both to literature and to psycho-analysis.

I do not have space here to cover fully Edel's persuasive arguments, or to evaluate the examples he cites—the symbolism in Willa Cather's novels, Robert Louis Stevenson's childhood feeding problem, or Ernest Jones's descriptions of Freud. Of course, Edel puts some of his theories into practice in his own great life of Henry James. For instance, Edel discusses the moot question of why James never married, and the compelling influence on him of the relationship of his father and mother. A skeptical reader might ask whether it may not have been more complicated than Edel suggests. He would reply that James's latent homosexual inclinations did not show up until his late years, and thus could not be brought into the early analysis.

In a recent letter Edel describes his method this way: "My entire biography takes its shape and form from my constant attention to the emotional content of James's life. The quest for the feelings contained in letters and his work is based of course on certain fundamental psychological premises, the most important being that art often takes its impulse first from the emotions, and only afterwards does the rational side of man intervene."[33] To those who reproach him for not sufficiently describing the social world in which James moved, Edel replies that his subject moved in that society as "a sentient being," and this capacity for feeling and not necessarily his environment, provides the needed clues.

Edel accepts Freud's theory of the significance of slips of the pen, and builds up an entire chapter from James's writing 1865 several times in a letter he was writing in 1884, and saying 65 when he wanted to say 85. As Edel comments, "This slip was a clue: it denoted an emotional involvement with '65 and set me to examining the meaning of that year in his life." Numerous interpretations in Volume IV would have been impossible had it not been for Edel's psychological orientation—the perception of James's depression behind his frequent euphorias and the meaning of his stories about little girls, etc.

Edel firmly believes that an author's works, if properly understood, can be of immense use to the biographer in interpreting psychological themes. For example, there is the relationship of James and Conrad. Conventional biographers would stress either James's occasional coldness to Conrad or the expressions of affection in certain of their letters. Edel tries to probe for the reason behind these apparent changes. As he describes it, "By my study of James's feelings, as expressed in letters, I saw that Conrad made James uneasy; and the uneasiness seemed to come from their difference in temperament. So I wrote my chapter in this way—choosing Conrad's *Heart of Darkness* and James's *The Beast in the Jungle* as indicative of the temperamental differences; both stories treat analogous themes and even have analogous imagery—but with enormous differences."

With many of Edel's points I agree completely. His interpretations are not casual speculations, but are based in each instance on a long and intricate chain of psychological evidence, derived from a mass of documents. In Henry James he had a perfect subject for such analysis. Biographers with different subjects might find it much more difficult. And still there is the problem of how much space should be given to lengthy analyses of character, even using nontechnical language. There is, too, the question of whether we can ever assume that what has been worked out gives the whole story. To which Edel concurs and quotes James, "The whole of any thing is never told."

Every reader of biographies will be struck by interpretations which appear reasonable, and others more dubious. A friend recently suggested to me that an instance of the former might be Justin Kaplan's *Mr. Clemens and Mark Twain* (1966), where he shows that Clemens, while he criticized the materialism of his age, was himself a son of his age who lived extravagantly and believed he had a right to be rich. Frustrated by some of his bad investments, he also blamed his publishers for mismanaging his literary profits. Kaplan makes clear that Clemens was a man imbued with the American dream in the later nineteenth century, certain that, even though an author, he ought to be rich like the businessmen of the era.

On the other hand, some of Irvin Ehrenpreis's suggestions about Swift, my friend confessed, he did not find quite so acceptable. In his *The Personality of Jonathan Swift*[34] Ehrenpreis argues, quite persuasively, that Swift's relationship to the women in his life resembled that of a father to his daughter or of a brother to his younger sister. The same author in the second volume of his life of Swift, when he comes to certain other bonds, is not so convincing. For instance, he argues that Swift not only viewed Sir William Temple as a father figure, but also regarded Harley (Lord Oxford) in the same light, though Harley was only six years older. Bolingbroke, probably because he was eleven years younger, is seen as a kind of surrogate son.[35] To some readers such interpretations appear to make too much of identifications and to overstress the idea that one's friendships are likely to be based on a "father image" or a "son image."

Another way of handling the problem can be illustrated by Constantine FitzGibbon's *Life of Dylan Thomas* (1965), where the reasons for his heavy drinking are discussed.[36] FitzGibbon provides a number of possible sources for Thomas's weakness—it was caused by the acute mental pressures that go with the act of creation; drinking gave him a new vision of the world; he tried to perpetuate the myth of the *Enfant Terrible*; he drank in self-defense when with distinguished people; he habituated bars because of his love of company. In the end FitzGibbon leaves it to the reader to choose the most plausible explanation. Although refusing to commit himself, he does try to assemble all the evidence and to present every possible kind of interpretation. The reader is thus provided with a background for judgment. On the other hand, critics might reply that by refusing to take a definite stand FitzGibbon is abrogating his responsibility. He could have consulted experts, even spent some days in an alcoholic clinic. As the one who should know most about his subject's inner motives, he owes it to his readers to indicate which he thinks is the most likely.

There is, of course, a third method—avoiding lengthy psychological explanations, whether or not technical terms are used, yet presenting to the reader all the relevant evidence without setting up alternative choices. In order to do this the biographer must himself be always aware of what others might do with the same evidence. He is still required to be acquainted with modern psychological theories, so that he can recognize significant details when they appear. Without ever using such terms as Oedipus complex, mother fixation, or death wish, his account must include all details which might bear on these themes. If the reader with sufficient grounding in analytical methods wishes to make his own interpretation, he can do so. At the same time another reader, uninterested in such evaluations, is not distracted by a succession of technical terms, which may have become out of date, or a possibly dubious character evaluation. At least the author has not placed any annoying barriers in his way.

One personal example may illustrate what I mean. As I was writing my study of the young Johnson, it became obvious that as

3. The Welsh Farmhouse ஓ The mystery of Broadley's vague footnote had actually been cleared up that first afternoon on the lawn at Brynbella. But through a second strange coincidence my cousin and I were led at once into another experience even more exciting.

When in the 1790's the Piozzis had built Brynbella, on top of the hill overlooking the Vale of Clwyd, they had decided to give up the old family home, Bach-y-graig, which stood down by the stream. A fine prospect, Mrs. Piozzi must have thought, was worth more than family sentiment. And so the old Elizabethan house had been torn down early in the nineteenth century. The coach house which remained was turned into a farmer's cottage. I knew all this from Broadley's book. Although there could be no Piozzian relics at what was left of Bach-y-graig, merely from curiosity Bob and I wanted to go by to take some pictures. But when we casually mentioned our intention, the ladies advised us to stay away. There was nothing to see, we were told, and besides, the property was now owned by a wild Welsh farmer named Roberts who resented intrusion. A nonconformist in both religion and politics, the farmer was in constant warfare with the local gentry. Refusing to allow any hunting over his property, he took pot shots at any strangers who chanced to come on his land. We were thus more likely to be greeted by a shotgun blast than any kind welcome.

All this only increased our determination to see Mrs. Piozzi's old property. After all, we were out for adventure as well as information, and the farmer's aim, we suspected, was probably not very accurate, or his quickness on the trigger as dangerous as the ladies insisted. And so the next day, after lunch at Miss Mainwaring's, and saying nothing about our plans to our agreeable hosts, we cycled down the hill to see what was left of Bach-y-graig. Yet despite our blithe air, it must be confessed that we approached the farmhouse with some uneasiness, being careful to keep a wary eye for any ambush.

No one was visible in the fields, but near some outbuildings we spotted a farm hand, who bluntly said that the owner was "up to house." There, the silence was slightly ominous. As we came near, we noted with casual interest how the former archway of the stables, through which coaches had passed for centuries, had been changed into a front door when the building was turned into living quarters. Like the original house, the stables had been built of Dutch bricks, better than native in the early sixteenth century, so that the old and new construction were easily distinguishable. Built in the shape of an "L," the house had kitchens and work-rooms in the rear extension.

Leaving our bicycles by two haystacks, we walked to the front door and rang the bell. No answer. I rang again and then knocked. Still no answer. I knocked again, somewhat louder. Not a sound. All was hushed in the calm of the setting sun.

"Nobody's home," I concluded, with perhaps a touch of relief. Though the prospect of braving the wild Welshman had sounded thrilling when we were on top of the bryn, I was beginning to wonder just how we would explain our visit. So I called to Bob, who had been busily snapping pictures of the house and farm buildings, that we had seen all we needed and had better go back to Brynbella for tea. And there, but for my enterprising companion, the adventure might have ended.

By this time, Bob had disappeared behind the house, and shouted to me that he heard voices. I called back not to disturb anybody, but when Bob failed to return I followed him to the rear door. Through a window we could see people having tea in a back room. Upon our knocking, a woman answered, and when I asked to speak to the owner, she showed us into a parlor.

In a few minutes the farmer appeared, large and red-faced, with a choleric expression, dressed for the fields with an open shirt. His name, Robert Roberts. As best I could I tried to explain the reason for our unexpected appearance at Bach-y-graig. I was writing about the life of an eighteenth-century lady who had once owned his property.

"Why?" he asked glumly. "What's so different about her from any other woman?"

Patiently, I tried to explain that I thought her a fascinating writer, and that she had been friendly with many important people.

"Was she any better woman than any other?" he grumbled.

I could not claim that she was. But she was more interesting.

He refused to admit that possibility. When I went on to say that she was the one who had built the beautiful house, Brynbella, at the top of the hill, he showed the first signs of recognition.

"I've heard she was a bad 'un. Havin' that old man always visitin' her."

So much for Mrs. Piozzi's local reputation as a friend of Dr. Johnson! The fact that Johnson had been dead for ten years before Brynbella was built was disregarded, if known to anyone. In the Vale of Clwyd she was docketed as a bad woman.

"How do you spell the name you call her?" he finally asked.

"P.I.O.Z.Z.I." I spelled it out. "That was the name of her second husband, an Italian musician."

"But why do you say it the way you do? P-i-o-z-z-i is Pie'-o-zee."

No amount of explanation about the Italian pronunciation of double z as "ts" had any effect. He was unconvinced.

"It's Pie'-o-zee," he insisted, and for the remainder of our conversation I said it his way.

Without too much prodding he pointed out where the foundations of the original Bach-y-graig had been, and then showed us around his cottage, indicating just how the arched coach entrance had been bricked in to make a room, which was beautifully paneled with wood from the old house. When we had at last seen everything we wished, and asked permission merely to take a few more pictures, we thanked him and started for the door.

But Roberts had been repeating to himself the name "Pie-o-zee." Now he spelled it out again.

"Seems to me I've seen that somewhere lately," he said. "Wait a minute."

Muttering to himself, he searched awkwardly in a drawer, finally coming out with a large key. With this he unlocked the door of a small room nearby, which had evidently been long used for storage

—filled with broken-down furniture, picture frames, bric-a-brac and smashed ornaments. Apparently here was the accumulation of generations of family junk, which nobody had had time or inclination to destroy. At one side was a table piled high with stacks of dusty papers, magazines, and books.

Searching through this mass, the farmer finally pulled out a soiled parchment deed, which he passed over to me. It proved to be one from the eighteenth century, having the signature of Mrs. Piozzi. Pointing to the name, he asked if this was the lady I had been describing. I said that it was indeed her signature. But I was not much interested. It was quite natural for him to have old deeds to the property. A mere legal document of this sort was of little use to me. But he kept searching around in the mass of papers and finally dragged out a little red morocco note book and handed it to me.

"What might this be?" he asked.

Casually I opened it, and then I stared. Here was Mrs. Piozzi's handwriting. As I hurriedly turned over the pages my excitement mounted. I could see at once that this was her daily diary for 1815, filled to the brim with notes in her hand. Although no name appeared on the flyleaf, the diary was unmistakably hers. Then the farmer kept pulling out other diaries, and then an account book in a strange hand which I assumed to be Piozzi's. I almost exploded.

Looking back calmly after many years' experience, I can see that this was a major mistake on my part. I should have been blasé and unconcerned. I should have expressed polite interest but indicated that these were not really worth anything. Instead I kept blurting out that this was "valuable," that was "wonderful." Yet my reaction is understandable. After all these years there should not have been any manuscripts at Bach-y-graig. So I kept asking him where they had come from.

Gradually he gave me the facts. The papers were there, so far as he could tell, because they had been brought to the house sometime around the turn of the century by Major Edward Pemberton Salusbury, the grandson of Mrs. Piozzi's heir. About that time Brynbella, the family residence, had been rented to outsiders. While his wife and daughter lived elsewhere, the Major preferred to stay in the neighborhood, and took rooms with one of his tenant farmers at Bach-y-graig. While there in 1908 he died suddenly. Though his family returned and went through his effects at the farmhouse, some scraps had been left behind. These remained in a large wooden cupboard in the storeroom which had not been touched until this summer. Meanwhile the farm and contents had been sold at public auction, at which time Roberts had become the owner. But he had never been curious to see what was inside the cupboard. And years had passed by.

Fortunately for me, however, the farmer's wife had long needed more storage space in her kitchen, and had been pestering her husband for permission to use the cupboard in the storeroom. A few weeks before we arrived on the scene he had finally given in. The cupboard had been emptied, and its contents thrown on the table in the storeroom. By chance, Roberts had noticed the deed containing the signature "H. L. Piozzi," and the strangeness of the name had made an impression which lasted for a few weeks.

Had we come to Bach-y-graig a month earlier, or a year, or ten years, he would have had no idea what was there. Had we come a year later, or five, he might well have forgotten, or the great stacks of what appeared to be rubbish might all have been destroyed. Some kind Providence brought me to that place exactly when I had to be there if Mrs. Piozzi's papers were to be found. I have never ceased to bless Mrs. Roberts for nagging her husband for that cupboard.

My open enthusiasm made him suspicious. The more I questioned him, the more his suspicions grew. When I wanted to see what else was on the table, he pushed us out of the storeroom and locked the door. He kept saying he didn't know who we were. How could he trust my assurances of honesty? And so he ushered us out of the house, with no promise to let us in again.

Imagine our excitement as we left Bach-y-graig to cycle up to Brynbella for another engagement with Mrs. Evans. The whole complexion had suddenly changed again. Yet at this stage it seemed better not to say anything about this new find to our friendly hosts, though to play ping-pong on the lawn, with our thoughts so fixed on other matters, was almost unbearable. When at last we were able to tear ourselves away, we cycled madly in to St. Asaph. Through supper and on into the night we talked and talked. As the Thomases listened sympathetically, we described every detail of our conversation with the farmer.

The pressing problem was what to do next, how to convince Roberts that we merely wanted to see what he had. There was also the problem of legal ownership, of what actual rights the farmer had to the manuscripts. And at the back of our minds was the possibility that there in the storeroom there might be material connected with Dr. Johnson.

In the end it was decided that the vicar should go out with me to assure Roberts of my honesty, and to urge him to let me make an inventory of the papers. All I asked now was to see what was there. The next morning, as we had planned, the vicar drove me to Bach-y-graig, where we found Roberts out in the fields. Then for what seemed an interminable time the two men talked in Welsh. Tormenting as it was not to have any idea of what was being said, there was nothing for me to do but wait patiently for the outcome. Fortunately my advocate was successful, and Roberts agreed to take me inside to see just what was in the storeroom. That it was a damp, lowering day, and thus not suitable for haying, was just one more piece of good luck.

A large table in the parlor was cleared, and there we carried armful after armful from the storeroom. Then the material was carefully separated into two piles, according to my own designation—one, "interesting," the other "uninteresting." Into the latter went nineteenth-century pictures, Victorian books, Salusbury family papers coming after the death of Mrs. Piozzi. In the "interesting" pile went anything from the eighteenth century, or directly associated with the lady.

As we proceeded, the rapidly expanding stack of manuscripts drew continued shouts of joy from me. I had not yet learned my lesson. For me everything was evaluated by what it contributed to my work on Mrs. Piozzi. For the farmer, I soon found out, the word "valuable" meant pounds, shillings, and pence. Inevitably, as the morning progressed, Roberts and I were being drawn farther and farther apart by our diverging scales of values. But of that I had no intimation at the time. Carried away by my own enthusiasm, I was oblivious to any other consideration except the thrill of each new discovery. And there were plenty of these.

Here was Gabriel Piozzi's birth certificate, which finally settled what had never been certain, the exact age of the lady's second husband. He was, I now found out, within a few months of her age, and not, as slander had insinuated, much younger. There were seven of Mrs. Piozzi's yearly diaries and six of her second husband's account books. There were packages of family business papers, deeds, etc., and a little book in French which she had owned when in her teens. It was a strange mixture of all kinds of things.

It was about the middle of the morning that we made our one important discovery—important, I should say, for the farmer and for me—a large blank book, having loose between its leaves a collection of autograph letters and separate manuscripts. Major Salusbury had been an ardent autograph collector, and this assortment may well have been his active file for sale or trade. Certainly it was a strange conglomeration, with signatures of the Duke of Wellington and Queen Victoria mixed in with those of minor eighteenth-century acquaintances of Mrs. Piozzi. Stray notes from Warren Hastings, Dickens, and Thomas Campbell were interposed between a copy of a poem by Thomas Gray and an invitation to the coronation of George IV. Leafing through the pages was like playing a guessing game of signatures.

What we had both been hoping to find was something specifically connected with Dr. Johnson, for he was the major figure who gave significance to the whole Piozzian group. Eagerly, then, we scanned each sheet. Suddenly I saw a handwriting which I knew well. It was Johnson's. Then there was another, and another. My enthusiasm burst all bounds, and Roberts and I beamed happily at each other in mutual congratulation. To be sure, none of the three sheets bore his signature, and Roberts had to take my word for it that the writing was his. But there could be no mistaking that characteristic hand. I had struggled through too many of Johnson's difficult manuscripts to have any doubts whatsoever.

Though there was no opportunity to read them through, I could see that they were all examples of his ghostwriting for the Thrales —a political advertisement to go in the newspapers, a draft of a begging letter to a nobleman concerned with one of Mrs. Thrale's charitable projects, something else having to do with the sale of the brewery after Thrale's death. They were all in Johnson's hand, and I was fairly certain that they were completely unknown. But what was even more exciting were letters of other people. Here was what turned out to be Fanny Burney's first letter to Dr. Johnson—a bit formal and hesitant, carefully worded and properly deferential. With it were two other notes by Fanny, one a delightful and characteristic message to Mrs. Thrale, in which she confessed to having fallen head over heels in love with Edmund Burke. Here, too, was a letter from Lucy Porter to Johnson, her stepfather, which more clearly revealed that maiden lady's character—her care about money, her dislike of being cheated, her quaint style—than anything I had ever seen before. Later on I was to discover that it was unique, being the only complete letter from Lucy Porter to Johnson that has survived.

There were other letters to Johnson from people whose names I did not then recognize—from the younger Thomas Coxeter, whom Johnson had saved from a press gang; from the schoolmaster Henry Bright; from Anne Welch, daughter of the well-known London nemesis of criminals, Saunders Welch. Much against my will, I was forced to pass hurriedly on. Yet it was natural to wonder what was the story behind each one. There were various letters to Mrs. Piozzi, some from well-known people like Edmund Burke and Arthur Murphy; some from obscure business agents or family friends. All, I was sure, must be unknown.

These were only some of the riches spread before me that day. At that stage I knew only enough to recognize the outstanding pieces, and not enough to be certain what was valuable and what was not. Although I was eager to copy as much as I could of the important material as it came to light, Roberts, who stayed at my side throughout, inexorably insisted that I merely jot down a few words describing each item. Occasionally he let me copy a sentence to indicate the nature of the contents.

Just the same, I was able to include a good deal of evidence. Even though ostensibly taking notes for a simple inventory, I made certain that should I never see the material again I would have recorded the most important facts. Tantalizing and frustrating as it was, it was a challenge to my skill at snap estimates and judicious excerpting.

All this took time. At noon we had a good lunch brought in by one of the family, and then through the afternoon, with the farmer still watchful, I continued to jot down notes at a furious pace. Tea time came, and I was still scribbling away. Not until 5:30, when my fingers were numb and cramped, did Roberts finally call a halt. With a deep sigh I stretched back in my chair and agreed to stop. Then sadly I helped him carry the piles of papers and books back into the storeroom and watched him close and lock the door.

Throughout the day at the back of my mind had been the problem of procedure—what steps I should urge upon the farmer. Obviously I needed expert advice myself before I made any further suggestions. Of course, the first thing would be to type a complete inventory from the notes that I had taken. That, at least, would give us something concrete to talk about. As I made ready to leave, I promised to send Roberts a copy of this list, and also agreed to talk to various scholars and librarians. Meanwhile I begged him not to say anything about the find until I returned in about three weeks. To this he readily agreed, and we parted in a friendly fashion.

Once back in St. Asaph, I found Bob and the Thomases eaten up by curiosity. Again there was an evening of excited talk, as we pored over my precious notes, and as I explained my guesses about the significance of each item.

ॐ

Discovering manuscripts is one thing; being able to study them at leisure, another. Behind the frantic excitement of the search always lurk such mundane considerations as ownership and commercial value. I was soon to find that the scholar adventurer must be as well equipped to talk business and to handle people as he is to decipher difficult handwriting. Clearly I could not hope to purchase the manuscripts myself, particularly with Roberts's inflated ideas of their value. The best possible solution from my point of view would be for the collection to go to some famous library like the British Museum or the Bodleian in Oxford. The chief dangers were that they might be bought by some collector who resented scholarly intruders, or sold at auction and thus widely dispersed. Always these two possibilities remained at the back of my mind.

I will skim hurriedly over the events of the next few months— talks with my Oxford advisers; another day at Bach-y-graig, three weeks later, checking my list under the watchful eye of the farmer; fruitless attempts to interest various librarians; a drive over from Manchester to examine the papers with Dr. Henry Guppy, Librarian of the John Rylands Library, and his subsequent meager offer, which infuriated Roberts. Affairs seemed to be going from bad to worse. The only progress came with my deepening friendship with Mrs. Evans at Brynbella. On my third trip I had told her in confidence of the Bach-y-graig discovery. Gradually I had been sending her all the books on Mrs. Piozzi that I could pick up from the second-hand stalls, and she was rapidly becoming an enthusiast.

One further complicating factor was my own uncertain health, the result of a bad cold and ear trouble which no specialist seemed able to cure. And so the autumn passed, with everything at an impasse. During the winter I tried to concentrate on other matters, and in Oxford and London kept at work studying the Mainwaring manuscripts and masses of other evidence. With spring the sun returned and with it my strength. Once again my thoughts strayed to the Vale of Clwyd and the unsolved problem there.

Then with no warning, early in May, a letter came from Mrs. Evans with the news that Roberts at Bach-y-graig was behaving queerly. She thought I had better drop everything and come at once to Wales. Of course, I did. At the Bodfari station, Mrs. Evans greeted me with an explanation of her disturbing message. Only a few days before, she had chanced to meet Roberts's wife on the road, and found her much upset. Her husband, she said, was not quite right. "He's been proper queer lately. We have a job to make him speak." So depressed had he become that she was taking him that day to see a doctor. Now, only this morning, Mrs. Evans had heard that the farmer was even worse and had not uttered a word for five days. He just sat morosely staring into space.

Though there could be no certainty, his family suspected that it was worry about the Piozzi papers which was at the back of his distress. He simply could not make up his mind whether he had a right to sell them, and, if so, how to find a purchaser who would not cheat him. Constant brooding over this and other matters had sapped his ability to make decisions, with the result that he was in a dismal condition.

Something had to be done immediately, in order to relieve the tension, and it was up to me to find the way. Still, there was the question of how safe it would be for me to approach the brooding farmer, who might blame me for his apparently unsolvable dilemma. Yet I knew that it was imperative that I see him the next day.

On this visit to the Vale I was to stay at Brynbella, and that evening Mrs. Evans and I canvassed all possibilities. Over and over we discussed various approaches. By this time she was determined to buy the collection for herself, if it could be secured at a fair price. But what was a proper figure? And how convince Roberts that it was? Even more important, how could I break through his present gloom and even make him listen to my arguments? There must be some way to stir him out of this dangerous lethargy.

It was with some trepidation that I walked down the next afternoon to Bach-y-graig. Even more than on that first visit I was uncertain of what I was facing. At least I was expected this time, for word had been sent ahead to let the family know I was coming.

Roberts himself, gloomy and silent, met me at the door. He made no motion whatsoever of welcome and merely stared at me with a fierce intensity. According to my well-laid plan, I then began to talk. And I talked and talked, never stopping for a moment. The one possible way, I had decided, was to ignore completely any lack of response, and at the same time to try to establish some bond of sympathy. Thus I chattered away about this and that, about what I had been doing since last in Wales, about anything that entered my head. In great detail I described my own recent illness, the trouble with my ear, elaborating on various distressing symptoms and futile methods of treatment. In the blackest colors I painted my own dejection of the late autumn and winter. I allowed myself scarcely time for breath. On I went, with a torrent of words, occasionally sneaking a glance at his face for some sign of interest. How long I talked I have no idea, for today that afternoon all seems like a strange, remote dream. All I can remember is that eventually I thought his expression began to relax, and there was some show of sympathy for my long tale of woe.

Still continuing my talking marathon, I began to edge my way into the doorway. When the chance came, I slipped past him into the hall. As he saw me slide by, he gave up with a shrug of resignation, and slowly led the way into the parlor.

Now, I could see, was the moment to make a break. As he sagged into a chair, I risked asking my first question:

"What kind of a winter have you been having?"

He struggled to answer. "Bad," he muttered. Yet all the bitterness of despair was in that one word.

"I've had a depression settle on me," he began. Then he poured out his own troubles. The weather in Wales had been vile. His sheep had been dying. Everything had gone wrong on the farm. And worst of all he still could not decide what to do about the papers. He had prayed about them constantly. He had talked to his minister. He simply could not make up his mind. The minister, a wise man, urged him to get the things out of his house, so that he could forget about them. But he was unable to do anything. No one would make him a proper offer. The sum Dr. Guppy had mentioned was insulting. He had thought some of selling the lot at Sotheby's. But at an auction how could he tell what the manuscripts would bring? He might have bad luck and get very little in the end. What should he do?

Here was my chance. Something, I said, must be done right away, not only for his state of mind, but for the good of everybody concerned. There was no use waiting any longer. Unfortunately, try as I might, I had been unable to find any library able to make the purchase. But Mrs. Evans, who lived in Mrs. Piozzi's old house, would like to have the papers back where they originally belonged. I stressed the fact that Mr. Evans was a business man, a Lysol manufacturer in Liverpool, and thus not one of the local gentry whom he so hated. To this he mumbled something to the effect that he had nothing personally against the Evanses. Of all his well-to-do neighbors they were the only ones he was willing to accept even grudgingly. I then stressed that they would be willing to pay much more than the Rylands Library had offered.

With that as a starting point, I tried to draw out of him how much he thought he ought to get. Still it was not easy. He shifted uneasily in his chair. Obstinately he refused to commit himself in any way. Finally, however, after long prodding, he did mutter in a low voice something about an outside figure which he felt the papers were worth. This was what I had been waiting for, and happily the figure he named was not unreasonable. Then trying not to show my elation, I said that I would try hard to see that he did receive that much. "Where?" he asked. From Mrs. Evans, I answered, but if not, from some other collector. With that I took my leave, promising to be back the next day to tell him what I had found out.

Jubilantly I hurried up the hill to Brynbella, where my host and hostesses were impatiently awaiting me. Out came the whole story, and we congratulated ourselves on this apparent break in the deadlock. As a shrewd business man, however, Mr. Evans was reluctant to offer the amount which Roberts had named, even though it was far from excessive. "If we do," he maintained, "he will only ask for more. We must start with something less and work up." On the other hand, after the long harrowing delay, I was in no mood for further haggling. Eagerly I urged that they be generous and offer the entire sum. But the Evanses remained adamant as to the amount to be offered, and since they represented my only real prospect, their decision had to be accepted. One thing I insisted upon—that after all my emotional involvement I be allowed to contribute part of the purchase price and get a few of the treasures.

Ceaselessly I kept ticking off all the possible ways of reaching a compromise figure which would be satisfactory to both parties. To be always caught in the middle was not a happy condition. Yet, strangely enough, the next morning my spirits were high. The day was perfect, warm and springlike, with a cloudless blue sky. The view across the Vale had never seemed lovelier.

About the middle of the afternoon I walked down again to Bachy-graig, where Roberts seemed positively delighted to see me. Again there began the interminable discussion. Over and over I rehearsed my carefully worked out arguments, all so patently obvious. The Evanses, I pointed out, thought that Dr. Guppy must have some clear idea about the value of the manuscripts. After all, he was an expert. Thus they were loath to offer much more than twice his bid. After a year of investigation this was the very best that I had been able to turn up for him. In a few months I would have to return to America, leaving him with no active agent to drum up interest. He would probably never find any better prospect than Mrs. Evans. Yet Roberts kept holding out for his price. At last I said that on my own responsibility I would agree to "split in other areas. It has been suggested, for example, that much more can be done in the study of handwriting. Not that graphologists in the past have ever been very convincing in their claims to be able to read character by this means. A man's style of writing may merely reflect his early school instruction. Nevertheless, certain emotional stresses can show up in his handwriting, and changes and variations during times of crisis may furnish a key to his inner moods.[39] Perhaps the omniscient computer will be put to good use here as well as in the measurement in personal documents of certain words and phrases indicating emotional tension.

For the biographer of living persons there are other exciting possibilities. Biologists now emphasize the functioning of the glands and the influence of genes.[40] One need hardly point out recent studies of prison populations where males have been found to have an extra chromosome, which, it is suspected, may account for their criminal tendencies. Ultimately will a biographer have to know how many chromosomes his subject has? And if so, will he be able to find out? Then there is the possibility that studies may establish correlation between blood types and character. One thing is certain: there will be new methods and far more material for him to absorb, and he must somehow learn how to fit all the disparate parts of the puzzle together into a believable and accurate portrait.

In this little book all that I have been able to do is to ask some pertinent questions, and to suggest certain difficulties. One may hope that the next generation of critics will come up with some acceptable answers.

Notes

Notes ❧

1. "OUTSIDE" VERSUS "INSIDE" RESEARCH

1. Vol. XVII of the Yale Walpole Edition, *Horace Walpole's Correspondence with Sir Horace Mann*, eds. W. S. Lewis, Warren Hunting Smith, and George L. Lam (New Haven, 1954), xxiii, lii.

2. *The Complete Letters of Lady Mary Wortley Montagu*, ed. Robert Halsband (Oxford, 1965), I, xiv–xvii.

3. J. L. Clifford, "The Authenticity of Anna Seward's Published Correspondence," *Modern Philology*, XXXIX (November, 1941), 113–22. To be sure, Miss Seward had never been a wholehearted admirer of Johnson. See her "Benvolio" letters in *Gent. Mag.*, LVI (February and April, 1786), 125–26, 302–4.

4. The original manuscript is now in the Berg Collection of the New York Public Library at 42nd Street. Work has begun on deciphering crossed-out passages and removing pasted sheets, but it is a very slow and difficult process.

5. See Kenneth Povey, "The Text of Cowper's 'Letters,'" *Modern Language Review*, XXII (January, 1927), 22–27.

6. *The Works of Mrs. Chapone* (London, 1807).

7. See J. L. Clifford, "Some Problems of Johnson's Obscure Middle Years," *Johnson, Boswell and Their Circle: Essays Presented to L. F. Powell* (Oxford, 1965), p. 106.

8. For an account of Michael Holroyd's experiences when beginning his biography of Lytton Strachey see "Biographer's Progress," *Twentieth Century Magazine*, No. 1036 (Spring, 1968), 9–14.

9. The story was told me originally by Susanne Nobbe. See also Anna Theresa Kitchel, *George Lewes and George Eliot* (New York, 1933), p. xii, where she gives the details.

10. See J. L. Clifford, "A New Johnson Correspondent," *TLS*, 30 May 1952, p. 368; and *The Letters of Samuel Johnson*, ed. R. W. Chapman (Oxford, 1952), III, 338–40.

2. THE VAGUE FOOTNOTE

1. The manuscripts were sent to the Taylorian Library, of which L. F. Powell was librarian, and I was allowed to use everything I pleased. They were sold at Sotheby's on 23 June 1969, and the "Children's Book" is now in the possession of Mrs. Donald Hyde, who plans to edit it. The five-volume set of Piozziana owned by the Mainwarings is now at Harvard, and the letters to the Williams family are in the possession of William Dawson in Pall Mall.

3. THE WELSH FARMHOUSE

1. Mrs. Evans died during the Second World War, and her manuscripts are now in the National Library of Wales in Aberystwyth.

4. THE PARALYZED OLD LADY

1. A shorter version of this story may be found in Richard D. Altick's *The Scholar Adventurers* (New York, 1950), pp. 118–21.

2. The Adam Collection was later purchased by the Donald F. Hydes, and this letter is now at "Four Oaks Farm" near Somerville, N. J.

5. A FEW OTHER CASES

1. *Life*, II, 338–39.
2. See Katharine C. Balderston, *The History and Sources of Percy's "Memoir of Goldsmith"* (Cambridge, 1926).
3. For all the details see *Dr. Campbell's Diary of a Visit to England in 1775*, ed. from the MS. by J. L. Clifford, with an Introduction by S. C. Roberts (Cambridge, 1947).
4. *Ibid.*, p. x.
5. *Ibid.*, pp. xiii–xv; and George Birkbeck Hill, *Talks about Autographs* (London, 1896), pp. 49–53.
6. Charles Welsh. See also John Taylor, *Records of My Life* (London, 1832). Apparently in the mid-nineteenth century the manuscript autobiography of Francis Newbery was still in the possession of the family.
7. Stuart Piggott, *TLS*, 13 June 1929, p. 474.
8. See Howard P. Vincent, "The Childhood of Henry Fielding," *Review of English Studies*, XVI (October, 1940), 438–44.
9. For some general considerations see F. A. Pottle, "Notes on the Importance of Private Legal Documents for the Writing of Biography," *Proceedings of the American Philosophical Society*, CVI (1962), 327–34.
10. Geoffrey Beard, *Georgian Craftsmen and Their Work* (London, 1966).
11. I owe this information to Professor Calhoun Winton of the University of South Carolina.

6. TESTING AUTHENTICITY

1. Jacques Barzun and Henry F. Graff discuss this matter in detail in *The Modern Researcher* (New York, 1957), pp. 88–175, and suggest various questions to be asked about each piece of evidence. For some interesting examples, see Rebecca West, *Ending in Ernest* (New York, 1931), pp. 161–68; and Wallace Notestein, "History and the Biographer," *Yale Review*, XXII (March, 1933), 549–58.
2. See *Philological Quarterly*, XXXI (July, 1952), 300; Lewis M. Knapp, *Notes and Queries* (April, 1953), p. 163; and *Modern Language Quarterly*, XIV (June, 1953), 228.
3. See *Letters of Laurence Sterne*, ed. L. P. Curtis (Oxford, 1935).
4. "Getting at the Truth," *Saturday Review*, 19 September 1953, pp. 11–12, 43–44.
5. Described in my *Young Sam Johnson* (New York, 1955), pp. 270–71, 252.
6. Cf. *Dr. Campbell's Diary* (Chapt. 5, note 3), pp. 75, 129; and *Boswell: The Ominous Years*, eds. Charles Ryskamp and F. A. Pottle (New York, 1963), pp. 123–24. Addison's timidity was proverbial. See J. Roderick O'Flanagan, *Lives of the Lord Chancellors of Ireland* (London, 1870), II, 8.
7. *Ibid.*, Campbell, pp. 76, 130; *Boswell*, p. 144; *Life*, II, 356.
8. *Ibid.*, *Boswell*, p. 135; *Campbell*, pp. 77, 131.
9. *Johnsonian Miscellanies*, ed. G. B. Hill (Oxford, 1897), I, 189.
10. *Life*, IV, 347.
11. *Life*, with marginal annotations by H. L. Piozzi, ed. Edward G. Fletcher. 3 vols., Limited Editions Club (London, 1938), III, 401. Two separate editions are used: a copy of the 8th edition (1816), now in the Harvard Univ. Library; and of the 5th edition (1807), now in the Hyde collection.
12. *Ibid.*, III, 31; *Life*, III, 325.
13. *Ibid.*, III, 183; *Life*, IV, 72.

14. *Ibid.,* I, 33; *Life,* I, 68.

15. *Ibid.,* I, 140; *Life,* I, 210.

16. Notestein, see note 1. As an example of how people who attended the same event can give very different accounts of what happened, see *New York Times Book Review,* 5 March 1961, p. 42; 26 March, p. 41. One of the correspondents remarked that the episode was "enough to make one ponder anew the age-old question: Where lies the truth?"

17. *Lives of the Poets,* ed. G. B. Hill (Oxford, 1905), III, 7–8.

18. Maurice Johnson, "A Literary Chestnut: Dryden's 'Cousin Swift,'" *PMLA,* LXVII (December, 1952), 1024–34. Also pp. 1232–40.

19. For some entertaining examples see *The Historian as Detective: Essays on Evidence,* ed. Robin W. Winks (New York, 1969).

20. For a justification of conflation of anecdotes, see Frederick B. Tolles, "The Biographer's Craft," *South Atlantic Quarterly,* LIII (October, 1954), 514.

7. FORM—TYPES OF BIOGRAPHY

1. See Tolles, "The Biographer's Craft," pp. 508–20; also Mary Purcell, "The Art of Biography," *Studies* (Dublin), XLVIII (Autumn, 1959), 305–17; and John A. Garraty, "How to Write a Biography," *South Atlantic Quarterly,* LV (January, 1956), 73–86.

2. See Leon Edel, "That One May Say This Was the Man: The Biographer Must Blow the Breath of Life into Inert Bits of the Past," *New York Times Book Review,* 24 June 1956, pp. 1, 12.

3. For these and other accounts of a biographer's search for evidence see Appendix of my *Biography as an Art* (London, 1962), pp. 242–47.

4. *TLS,* 10 August 1969, p. 749.

5. *Literary Biography* (Toronto, 1957), pp. 90–98.

6. See *TLS,* 30 October 1969, pp. 1–2, for a very discerning review, which explains many of his techniques. For a different reaction see P. N. Furbank, "The Biographer as Trainer," *The Listener,* 18 December 1969, pp. 860–61.

7. Holroyd now plans to separate the material into two parts, one concentrating on the life, the other on criticism of Strachey's works.

8. THE BIOGRAPHER'S INVOLVEMENT

1. Gouverneur Paulding in *The Reporter,* 9 January 1958, p. 46.

2. See Chapt. 7, note 5.

3. *Lives of the Poets,* ed. G. B. Hill (Oxford, 1905), I, 156. Mrs. Victoria Sullivan first pointed this out to me.

4. Michael Holroyd, *Lytton Strachey: A Critical Biography* (London, 1967–68), II, 415.

5. See Chapt. 6, note 4.

6. Cf. James Anthony Froude, *Thomas Carlyle* (London, 1884); and Elizabeth A. Drew, *Jane Welsh and Jane Carlyle* (New York, 1928).

7. *The Letters of Sir Walter Scott,* ed. H. J. C. Grierson (London, 1932–37), I, lxxvii.

8. *The Listener,* 27 October 1966, p. 612.

9. See Chapt. 6, note 4.

9. HOW MUCH SHOULD A BIOGRAPHER TELL?

1. "How Much Should a Biographer Tell? Some Eighteenth-Century

Views," *Essays in Eighteenth-Century Biography,* ed. Philip B. Daghlian (Bloomington, Ind., 1968), pp. 67–95.

   2. See Introduction to *Biography as an Art: Selected Criticism, 1560–1960,* ed. J. L. Clifford (London, 1962).

   3. XIX (October, 1758), 386. The ascription of authorship is given in B. Nangle, *The Monthly Review, First Series* (Oxford, 1934), p. 147.

   4. There is an excellent modern edition, edited by Robert J. Gemmett (Cranbury, N. J., 1969).

   5. *A Poetical and Congratulatory Epistle to James Boswell* (London, 1786). Included in *The Works of Peter Pindar,* new edition (London, 1812), I, 324, 330.

   6. N.S. VII (January, 1792), 3–4; Nangle, *Second Series* (Oxford, 1955), p. 92.

   7. *TLS,* 12 April 1963, p. 248.

   8. Alfred Kazin, *Vogue,* 15 February 1968, p. 46.

   9. Louis Simpson, *Book World,* 13 July 1969, pp. 1, 3.

   10. George Steiner, *New York Times Book Review,* 22 June 1969, pp. 5, 18. Burling Lowrey recently wrote to *Book World* (26 October 1969): "Haven't we suffered long enough from a surfeit of over-researched, padded, trivia-ridden tomes that have passed for definitive literary biographies?"

   11. "Boswell's University Education," *Johnson, Boswell and Their Circle* (Oxford, 1965), pp. 230–53.

   12. Manuscript in my possession. See note 1, p. 87.

   13. W. Roberts, *Memoirs of Hannah More* (London, 1834), II, 16.

   14. LXXIV (May, 1786), 373–74; Nangle, p. 209.

   15. Robert Anderson, *Life of Samuel Johnson,* 3d ed. (Edinburgh, 1815), p. 6.

   16. See Joseph W. Reed, Jr., *English Biography in the Early Nineteenth Century, 1801–1838* (New Haven, 1966), pp. 3, 130–31, etc.

   17. "How Much Should a Biographer Tell?" *Saturday Review,* XLVII (25 January 1964), 16–19. For some other modern discussions of the problem, see Wilfred Partington, "Should a Biographer Tell?" *Atlantic* (August, 1947), 56–63; J. Donald Adams, *New York Times Book Review,* 9 February 1964, p. 2.

   18. Lord Chandos, "O Tempora, O Moran!" *Spectator,* 27 May 1966, p. 657.

   19. Benedict Hoskyns, London *Times,* 27 April 1966, p. 13. The papers were filled with similar attacks.

   20. London *Times,* 25 April 1966, p. 11. There were other letters in the *Daily Telegraph.* For one analysis of the problem see Hector Bolitho, "The Doctor and the Biographer," *Texas Quarterly,* XI (Winter, 1968), 52–60, where the importance of medical facts is stressed.

   21. Lord Normanbrook, London *Times,* 24 May 1966, p. 13.

   22. See note 18.

   23. H. A. Williams, London *Times,* 27 April 1966, p. 13. Another paper commented: "Far from diminishing the Churchill legend, it enhances it."

   24. London *Times,* 2 May, p. 11.

   25. London *Times,* 16 May, p. 11.

   26. John Prince, London *Daily Telegraph,* 29 April 1966, p. 17; *TLS,* 2 June 1966, p. 485; *Indianapolis News,* 18 June 1966; John Grigg, *Manchester Guardian,* 23 May 1966, p. 8. See also Douglas Hubble, "Lord Moran and James Boswell," *Medical History,* XIII (January, 1969), 1–10.

27. See note 1.

28. *TLS,* 10 April 1969, p. 388.

29. For some of the details see Philip Magnus, *Gladstone* (New York, 1954), pp. 105-10, 245, 305, 345.

30. Erik H. Erikson, *Young Man Luther* (London, 1958); and *Ghandi's Truth* (London, 1969). Erikson, of course, is an experienced practicing psychiatrist.

31. Pp. 60-61; "The Biographer and Psycho-Analysis," *New World Writing,* No. 18 (Winter, 1961), 50-64; and "Literature and Biography," *Relations of Literary Study,* ed. James Thorpe (New York, 1967), pp. 57-72. See also *Toronto Quarterly,* XXVIII (April, 1959), 301-9; John A. Garraty, "The Interrelations of Psychology and Biography," *Psychological Bulletin,* LI (November, 1954), 569-82; and Willard M. Gaylin, "Psychoanaliterature: The Hazards of a Hybrid," *Columbia University Forum,* VI (Spring, 1963), 11-16.

32. Edel, *Literary Biography,* p. 60.

33. In a letter to me of 8 November 1969. See also Chapt. 7, note 6.

34. (1958), pp. 9-28.

35. *Swift: the Man, His Works and the Age* (London, 1967), II, 455, 457, 468.

36. Pp. 128-32.

37. *Young Sam Johnson,* p. 25.

38. Edmund Bergler, "Samuel Johnson's 'Life of the Poet Richard Savage'—A Paradigm for a Type," *American Imago,* IV (December, 1947), 42-63.

39. See Garraty (note 31), p. 575.

40. I owe this and other valuable suggestions to Professor Maurice Quinlan of Boston College.

Index

Index &

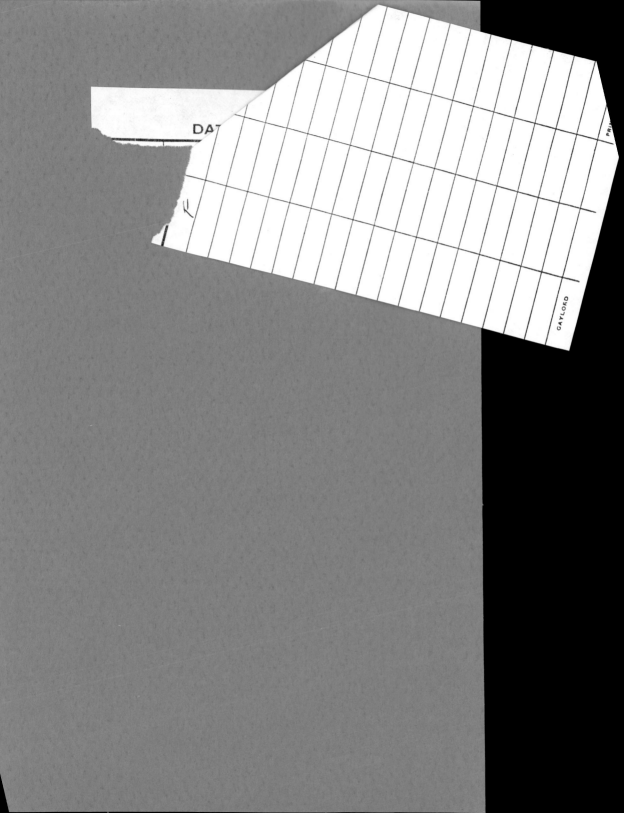

DAT

GAYLORD